T0208505

JOURNEY
BACK TO SELF

PENELOPE ROSE

BALBOA.PRESS
A DIVISION OF HAY HOUSE

This book is a work of non-fiction. Unless otherwise noted, the author and the publisher make no explicit guarantees as to the accuracy of the information contained in this book and in some cases, names of people and places have been altered to protect their privacy.

Scripture quotations marked NIV are taken from the Holy Bible, New International Version®. NIV®. Copyright © 1973, 1978, 1984 by International Bible Society. Used by permission of Zondervan. All rights reserved. [Biblica]

Balboa Press books may be ordered through booksellers or by contacting:

Balboa Press
A Division of Hay House
1663 Liberty Drive
Bloomington, IN 47403
www.balboapress.com
844-682-1282

Because of the dynamic nature of the Internet, any web addresses or links contained in this book may have changed since publication and may no longer be valid. The views expressed in this work are solely those of the author and do not necessarily reflect the views of the publisher, and the publisher hereby disclaims any responsibility for them.

The author of this book does not dispense medical advice or prescribe the use of any technique as a form of treatment for physical, emotional, or medical problems without the advice of a physician, either directly or indirectly. The intent of the author is only to offer information of a general nature to help you in your quest for emotional and spiritual well-being. In the event you use any of the information in this book for yourself, which is your constitutional right, the author and the publisher assume no responsibility for your actions.

Any people depicted in stock imagery provided by Getty Images are models, and such images are being used for illustrative purposes only.
Certain stock imagery © Getty Images.

Cover Artwork by Jacob Dawkins

Print information available on the last page.

ISBN: 979-8-7652-4786-0 (sc)
ISBN: 979-8-7652-4787-7 (e)

Library of Congress Control Number: 2023923508

Balboa Press rev. date: 01/03/2024

For Erica Perez, whose wise guidance, mentorship, and loyal friendship supported me through this journey, and lead me through the dark

Te Amo my sister

CONTENTS

PREFACE

This story starts with love. What else should any story be about once you really get down to the core of all things that mean anything in this life?

Love of one another, love of animals, love of
earth, creation, love of spirit, love of self.

This story starts with romantic love. Love that set me free. Love that sparked an awakening within me and met me at my depths, one that changed me forever. Love filled with passion and ecstasy and the deepest pain I ever imagined possible. A love few knew of until now. Love that broke my heart, and so vividly opened my eyes. One that shed light on the path I had been traveling all along. Love that kicked down the final door on my journey back to *self*.

A very crucial point to this story is to remember that *love* is the teacher here, (isn't it always?) This love and this kind of connection, soul recognition and deep admiration is where I invite you, my dear reader, to place your attention as we continue, not on my partner himself. I believe we made a soul agreement before entering this life to play the roles each of us played in this story. He wasn't my savior, as many fairytales programmed me to be looking for. He also wasn't my villain.

Many love songs, breakup songs, and movies in our culture teach codependence or place blame and victimhood. The girl ruined your life, or the guy rode in on a white horse and saved you. The Jerry McGuire *"you complete me,"* was really setting us up for failure in the true meaning of unconditional love and partnership. This, my friends, is a different story. This is a story of my mirror. A summer love that turned into the greatest lesson I've ever learned and the deepest healing I've ever known. Healing of what I believe to be generational pain that goes back centuries: self-worth.

Self-worth, in my case, is a synonym for self-love. The courage to speak my truth, honor my power, and to choose myself. To choose myself above all else, surrounded by a world that taught me from a very young age to *sacrifice* myself at all costs. A world that taught me to sacrifice myself for love, for acceptance, and for approval.

I'm choosing to share with you in this first chapter my greatest love because I feel with it, I was given a gift. This relationship and the awareness I was gifted around it is extraordinary and nothing short of divine. A relationship where time and space cease to exist. My partner has his own side of the story to tell, as his lessons mirror similarities, and maybe someday he will share with you. However, this one is mine.

This love was the catalyst that finally opened my eyes to the purpose of my life, to heal.

I believe I am here to heal generational curses of low self-worth so I can first experience life fully and freely and then assist others in their own healing. I believe I was gifted relationships in all forms beginning in childhood on to learn many perspectives, situations, and viewpoints so I could empathetically see all sides and have the knowledge and tools to support others in finding this courage within themselves.

The clarity I have been gifted is what I wish to share with you now. I have known the deepest and darkest levels of pain and confusion, never understanding why things happened the way they did in the moment, or why I had lived such extremes in a short amount of time. Everything happened exactly as planned is my belief, so I could be here sharing this perspective with you now. A perspective of understanding, one of non-judgement one of compassion and unconditional love to whatever you've been through.

When an author writes a non-fiction book, they are bottling up a lifetime of lessons and experiences they have in hopes to help you, teach you, save you time, and give you insights and cheat codes to assist in propelling you forward at an accelerated speed. This is my intention for you. I trust this book will find who needs it, and in the exact time they need it, when I'm here and long after I'm gone.

CRACKED OPEN

Our eyes locked across a circle of friends enthralled in a deep conversation. I'll never forget the moment. Standing in a circle at Top Golf, something chemically changed in my body as we saw each other for the first time. It wasn't really the first time. I had known him for about eight years without really knowing him at all. In truth, I never cared to know him before. We were in the same company so we would see each other and had even worked together a few times over the years. In total honesty, I admired the way he spoke, and he inspired me from afar. However, I thought he was arrogant and was fine with keeping my distance. We will call him Elijah, Eli for short.

We were at a VIP experience with our company this Friday night in April, downtown Cleveland. People were all around getting food and drinks, talking, and practicing their golf swings. I found myself in a small circle to the side of the food tables, listening as they were diving in on personal growth and spirituality. I had been exploring this world for years on my own, so I was happy to be included.

They were going round and round talking about books, retreats, experiences, coaches, plant medicine, and different things they were excited about. I stayed quiet, observing for most of the conversation, happily existing in the background, until I piped up quickly about something I was working on with my coach. His gaze lifted in my direction and his eyes locked with mine, as if finally finding their home. The world slowed down to a stop and blurred like a movie. My heart felt like it stopped beating for a moment and everyone and everything else completely disappeared as he continued to stare at me for what felt like an eternity. No words, we didn't need them. I remember thinking, "Did anyone else just see that!?"

Absolute panic set in. "WHAT *was* THAT!? *Am I crazy? HIM, of all people, no way. Absolutely not. He doesn't even date anyone? I don't even LIKE him. I'm overthinking this. There is just no way!*"

As much as I would like to put on a facade about being the *cool* girl in this story, that's just not the truth, and pinky promise If I'm going to bare my entire soul to you in this book I might as well be completely honest from the jump.

My internal monologue began a frenzy that would not give me an ounce of rest for the remainder of the weekend. Not many things in my world made sense, however, I was now sure of one thing. I *needed* to be near him, and thankfully (for the sake of my ego), he felt the same. We found any reason to speak to each other, to flirt, or to walk next to one another. I don't think either of us had any clue what was happening, but it didn't really feel like we had a choice in the matter, like magnets.

My best friend and her husband were walking beside me as we headed to the shuttle busses, when the driver came out to halt us. He directed only a few more of us to get on the first bus; the rest having to wait for the next one. "Three more," the driver said. My friend lightly guided me with her arm towards her husband and the first bus. "Perfect! She said, come on!" I felt my whole body come to a stop and I could feel Eli walking just a few steps behind me. I hesitated, looking at my friend I said, "you guys go ahead, I'll wait!" My eyes saying a lot more than my mouth. She grinned, understanding my telepathy, and headed to the first bus, leaving me behind. My internal monologue ERUPTED.

"WHAT DO YOU THINK YOU ARE DOING? He is not your boyfriend. You don't even know him! You can't just assume he will find his place right next to you! Great! Now he's going to think we are stalking *him*. Perfect, another fan girl!"

He was used to those, and ironically, I may have been one of the few who had never idolized or fantasized about him. We didn't even follow each other on social media. He was very successful in our company, hot, and popular. Racking my brain, I was trying to figure out how this person I had never even liked on a friend level for the past almost eight YEARS I was now pulled to so strongly I felt I couldn't possibly ride the fifteen minutes back to the hotel without him. Quicksand.

"Get a room my God!" blurted out a friend of mine at the after party the following night. She startled me back into reality because I was on another planet trying to figure out this whole situation in my head. "I'm sorry, what?" I asked her. "You and Eli!" I could cut the tension with a knife, Penelope! The way you two are looking at each other is even making me uncomfortable," she said, laughing. "So, I'm not making this up?" I asked frantically. I hadn't yet voiced my inner agony to anyone and was grateful she broke the silence.

"Um, absolutely not. I'm going to go chill in the room. Have fun tonight!"

She said as she squeezed me before walking off.

A large group of us walked to a bar, and I can't remember anything from that night except being absolutely smitten in every way. He invited me to sit with him while we ate, and when I climbed up on the barstool, our legs touched, starting at the knees and again our eyes locked, silently understanding we didn't need any verbal confirmation for whatever was happening. It was mutual. Once our legs touched, neither one of us moved a muscle for the next hour and a half.

The remainder of the event weekend was encounter after encounter. Any excuse to say something to the other, flirting, teasing, staring, and mainly questioning my sanity.

"Don't look at me like that," he warned with intense eyes and a kind smile as he followed me out of the event that Sunday. "I'll look at you however I want to," I replied, accepting the challenge. Sassy is what he always calls me. Sadness surfaced as time dwindled and the weekend was ending. Would we go back to separate lives? Would we talk before the next event months away? We had communicated a LOT without saying anything at all, and I wondered what was happening in that beautiful head of his. What was happening in mine was the reality of how different our lives were; I was a single mom, and he spent months out of the country.

"I'm excited about the Mike concert tonight," he said. My eyes and heart lit up. "You're going to that, really?" I asked in disbelief trying to hide my excitement. He then went on to share this long history and "love" of the artist I was absolutely obsessed with who just so happened to have a concert down the street that night. I had VIP meet and greet passes and had been waiting for this concert for months. Here, I was most definitely a fan girl. You could find me front row, screaming every word, having this man sign my Dunks with a sharpie. Whereas Eli was going with a group of twenty people on his team and planned to vibe in the back, we were not the same lol. "Well, maybe I'll see you there," I smiled calmly, while internally feeling the most alive I had in a very long time.

"Just do it!" There she was again. My internal monologue coming in hot, interrupting the best concert I had ever been to. Screaming every word, having the time of my life with my best friend and all I could think about was seeing him. "Just go back there. Then WHAT? Awkwardly stand beside him and try to explain why I would leave the front row in the middle of the concert to walk around the back of the crowd and pretend it surprised me to find him? Brilliant plan!" I thought.

I battled the screaming voice inside urging me to go for two more songs, until I gave in, "FINE! "I'll go to the bathroom, I'll be able to fight my way back up here, if I see him on the way I'll say hi," I thought, convincing myself I wasn't insane.

As I pushed my way through the crowd, there he was, right up against the back wall; he looked up at me and his eyes tried to hide the same butterflies and joy I was fighting.

"Five more concerts," he teased me over the roar of the crowd. "I'll tell you in five more concerts." Playfully, I begged for him to tell me when I was fine with waiting. Yes, I wanted to know this secret he was holding on to, but I wanted the five concerts with him more.

I didn't leave his side for the rest of the night. Months later he told me he stood at the back of the concert thinking, "If she comes back here, it's over," and he was right. That night was the beginning of eight months that changed my life.

We spent two-to-six hours on Facetime every night for the next week, half the time just staring at each other. Sharing songs, stories, laughing and losing every ounce of sleep. Exactly a week later, we went back to the same concert in Michigan this time. I had tickets and a hotel room with a girlfriend of mine he was friends with, and he and his cousin (who also doubled as his best friend and roommate) grabbed tickets to join us. We couldn't wait to experience the concert again and it served as the perfect first date. No one has ever held me as tightly as he did that night, dancing in the crowd.

"I've been waiting seven years for this," he whispered to me in the midst of the music. His body was behind me, arms wrapped around my frame, and his face was gently brushing against my left cheek. It surprised me to hear him voice it, but I knew exactly what he meant. Although I didn't understand why, and had never thought of him before, I too felt that I had been waiting for lifetimes. It was the beginning of something so ethereal, so difficult to explain.

Our friends ran ahead after the four of us grabbed pizza on the walk back to the hotel, trying their best to give us time alone. The cold air and his warm hands are burned into my memory. We reached the hotel and just before walking in the door, he grabbed me and turned me to face him, pushing me up against the building, so gently grabbing my face, he pressed into me and kissed me. "Finally," I thought. I'm hearing a *Novo Amor* playlist as I type this, and it couldn't be a better soundtrack to the moment. All that you dream of, better than any movie I had ever seen, *magic*.

My eyes were heavily fighting sleep laying on his chest in my hotel room. I had never felt safer. The vibration from his voice was so comforting as he was talking to our two friends sitting in the room

with us. "Do you want to run to the car with me? I forgot something."
I heard our friends awkwardly creating a quick plan to give us a few
minutes alone before parting ways till morning. "Stay," I whispered
when I heard the heavy hotel door close, not wanting him to go. "Not
tonight," he laughed, knowing he was committed to going back to his
room. "I just want to sleep," I argued. "We have plenty of time," he
said. I looked up at him and realized what they meant when they say,
"the eyes are the door to the soul."

His eyes were full of tears and his voice cracked as he brought my
biggest fear to life. "I don't want to hurt you," he said.

What he meant was "I don't want to hurt," because he knew what
I knew. We loved each other already, and this was either going to be
the greatest love story of all time, or completely destroy us.

"You won't," I said. I kissed him, desperately hoping I was right.

I had my fair share of relationships, and I had said I love you
many times, but this was something different. Something beyond.

(I am fully aware how dramatic this may sound, however every
part of this is the truth. I couldn't make it up if I tried. We were both
born hopeless romantics, and this was something magical. Doing my
best to translate into language, however, energy is hard to translate,
especially energy of this caliber.)

The memories I have of the next eight months could fill the pages
of their own novel. However, for the sake of this story, I'll sum it up
in a few paragraphs.

Every day we had together was better than the last. He was so
beautiful. It startled him the first time I told him that, but no other
words would suffice. Our connection was stronger than anything I
had ever experienced for sure, but also stronger than any I had ever
seen anywhere else as well. Seeing the candlelight reflection in his
eyes as we lay staring at each other for hours. Beach night after beach
night, watching the sunset fade into a starlit sky. Staring at the moon,
feeling my heart open. Windows down with his hand on mine, the
summer breeze blowing through my hair. Pizza on the hood of the
G-wagon at midnight, in late July.

The main person who knows our story best is Eli's cousin because he was with us a lot of the time. House projects, countless breakfast, and gym dates; he even wrapped my son's Christmas presents for me. The three of us have so many memories in that house, and I got the blessing of gaining another brother amid gaining this new love.

Eli and I would meditate and pray together in the backyard watching the deer. He would read to me and carry me from the couch when I would fall asleep without fail, five minutes into a movie. Country concerts and baseball, bubble bath giggles with an ocean view in Mexico.

Three AM nights in the kitchen laughing our faces off and slow dancing to a blaring Dermot Kennedy through the speakers. Smoking a blunt and making pancakes while planning all our business ventures. The absolute obsession and desire to feel each other's skin, and a sex life only one could dream, existed. A touch or even a glance would leave us defenseless to one another.

"I love you," I said, feeling the rush of fear run through my body after the words fell from my lips. It was a few months in, and I had known for a long time. It got to the point of feeling absurd that we hadn't said it yet. He stared at me deeply, not saying a word, and I felt the panic arise. "You don't have to say anything, you don't have to say it really, you…" "shhhh" he said. "Just let me be here with you." I took a deep breath and could feel my nerves relax as his eyes filled up with tears, mine following soon after. "I know," he said. "You don't have to say it for me to know. We already say it. I haven't said it out loud because it just seems so.."

"Like it doesn't even touch it," I said. "Exactly, it's so much deeper… words can't…" his words trailing off. "I knew I loved you at the concert. It wasn't a falling in love. It was like remembering, like my soul had finally found yours," he said.

The long-distance longing for one another when one was traveling. The painful goodbyes and the emotional welcome-homes. Songs, and notes, seven-hour-long FaceTimes. I loved him with every fiber of my being. I understood poetry; I understood songs I hadn't before; I believed in soulmates, past lives, and magic. We could feel each other even when we were across the world. He was smart; he was so weird, just like me. We liked to keep to ourselves. We are both introverts, but I think it was mainly because we didn't want to share our time with anyone else. It was sacred.

We sparked massive spiritual awakenings within each other, and every day, we were uncovering something else.

Neither of us expected this love, and we came up on roadblocks every week or two. When a connection is this spiritual in nature, and accelerates at such a speed, decisions, problem solving, hard conversations, and compromises get to be made at every corner. With every "I love you so much," and every laugh, came an equal number of tears. Every day was a choice to continue. Continuing in this relationship was cracking us both open and bringing to the surface every insecurity and fear we had ever buried underneath. Every childhood trauma, every past wound, every belief we needed to unlearn, every unhealed part of ourselves was being opened, and it was far from easy. Love is a healer; however, love is also a teacher.

He was the most beautiful mirror for me, and I had a choice to face it or run from it, as did he. No matter how much you love someone or how strong a connection, all the stuff brought to the surface has to be faced for a connection to grow into a true, sacred partnership. Rumi has this quote:

"You have to keep breaking your heart until it opens," and that is exactly what was happening.

The love I had for him was enough to crack my heart open. A feeling so *Free*, while simultaneously leaving me the most vulnerable I had ever been.

More on this story later. For now, I invite you to journey back with me to where this all began. Where all our journeys begin, *childhood*.

INTRODUCTION

I've studied human psychology endlessly for about ten years at the time of writing this book, and what I have found is most psychologists believe that by the age of seven, the majority of our beliefs about ourselves and the world around us are formed. Something impactful happens, and we draw lines in the sand forever being changed by the experience. The experiences we have, what we decide to make these experiences mean, and the major influences of authority figures around these experiences greatly affect our beliefs. Our beliefs then form into thought patterns that greatly affect our habits, and these habits, most of us then carry subconsciously into adulthood, therefore affecting our entire future; Intense, I know.

There is so much information taken in, and during this time, we are incredible little sponges. There are positive belief patterns, and of course, we all pick up some beliefs that don't serve us. The negative belief patterns form from a wide range of experiences. These, for example, could be something an adult said to you, a learned behavior, or something you witnessed that scared you. A heavy emotion you felt in response, a drastic life change, or a physical or mental trauma. The intensities and severities of these experiences differ from person to person. However, regardless of what they were, we all have some things to unpack, unlearn, and heal so that we can propel ourselves forward mentally, physically, and spiritually. The awareness of what these negative belief patterns are, how they affect us and our life choices, and where they originate from are a serious source of power.

Because like a weed overtaking our garden, the issues we face, and the negative belief patterns we repeat will never fully resolve if only ever managed at the surface. Surface level solutions could involve worldly distractions, addictions, and codependent relationships. Like in the garden analogy, we can cut the grass and spray pesticides all day, however unless taken at the root, the weed will never fully be gone. The first step in the healing process is awareness, and awareness, is the first major source of power. Because with awareness, we now have choice. To fully step into our power comes with the second step; The second step is doing the work to dig up our proverbial roots.

In this first chapter, we will cover the fundamental experiences I had between birth and seven years old, and the belief patterns I formed about myself, others, and how I functioned in relationship. For the sake of keeping on track, let's use the analogy of a backpack. Imagine entering life with a big empty backpack, and with each belief pattern, we will imagine a weight being added into the backpack, making it heavier and heavier to carry.

In the chapters following, I will share different relationships and experiences I've walked (or crawled) through where these belief patterns and habits showed up in a multitude of ways. In each chapter, I will share my story and lessons I learned from each experience. It is my belief reading my story will spark insights about your own life and awaken a new level of awareness inside of you. I also feel reading my story will resonate in a lot of ways, and you will find pieces of yourself in my experiences as I have had a wide range of them, and we are all a lot more similar than we think. Many of us face the same fears, same doubts, and same insecurities. We all just wear them differently.

I've created a resource workbook you can access for free on my social media accounts. Follow penelopesophiarose on Instagram and YouTube to access resources. There are reflections and journal prompts for each chapter. Choice number one; You can choose to read along with an open mind, and welcome whatever awareness comes up within you. You can choose to absorb the lessons I share from each experience and take what resonates. Choice number two will be to start digging up your own roots with the workbook. You can print it off and do it as you go along or read the book through once and come back to start your own *Journey Back to Self.*

I've read countless books, consumed a vast number of podcasts and YouTube videos over the years with an insatiable thirst for growth. They gave me so much knowledge, however, at some point I had to go inward and do the work *inside.* Nothing could compare to the life-changing shifts that this would cause. I had to put down everyone else's thoughts and lessons and gain the courage to face my own. You will learn from reading this book, but you will grow from answering the reflection questions and playing full out in each practice. Trust your intuition, you will know what you are ready for. Let's begin, shall we?

CHAPTER ONE

A NEW WORLD

I came screaming into this new and exciting world just two days short of a Valentine's baby. I see this fitting as love has always been my North Star, and the impetus of this book. Penelope was the name given to me by my parents. Penelope after my mother's late father Penn; my grandpa was my mother's favorite person, and he passed away right before my mom found out she was pregnant with me. She always says I saved her from her grief, forcing her to eat and take care of herself. Regardless of my sex, I was going to be a Penn. Sophia, my middle name; a middle name that was passed down from multiple generations on my mom's side, and Rose, carrying my father's lineage. My dad is one of seven children and a single mother. (Both my grandmas are tough as nails, and earth angels in their own right.) My grandpa left them when my dad was only seven years old, and because of that, family and being a provider has always been greatly important to him. My mother had escaped a very toxic and abusive relationship with my older brother's biological father prior to meeting my dad. Both of my parents were hotties in the 90s. They were one of those weird couples who kind of look like siblings, so when people ask me who I look like I just say "both".

They married, my dad adopted my older brother, and then they had me. I have photos of my mom kissing my cheeks, dressing me to the nines in the most ridiculous dresses covered in lace and ruffles, and photos sitting on my dad's lap with one of his hats backwards on my head. His smile lit up. Brown-Eyed Girl they both sing to me still to this day.

"You my brown eyed girl"- Van Morrison

I don't have any memories of my parents together, just the photos; they divorced when I was only three years old. This is the first experience that made its mark.

#1 DIVORCE

What is interesting about this was my parent's actual divorce was not traumatic, or even memorable for me to be honest. I never knew a world with my parents together. Growing up in two houses was normal for me and I was an optimistic and stress-free child. I spent most of my time outside, always very connected to nature, and loved playing in the dirt and riding my bike. I was also extremely girly and was a born performer; singing and dancing for everyone by the time I could talk. I was little miss fourth of July when I was four, would do ballet performances in the living room, and would proudly sing Twinkle Little Star to the crowd at my brother's baseball games.

When you're little, you grow up thinking everyone lives the same reality. Nothing about them not being together was a problem for me until I realized that my world looked very different from my peers.

The first grade was the first time I became aware that no one else in my class had divorced parents; No one had two houses, or stepparents. No one else had every other weekend schedule, step siblings, or had to pack a bag and say goodbye to their mom or dad for multiple days at a time. Humans on an instinctual level like to be a part of a tribe, and the realization I did not fit into the norms of the tribe was confusing, scary, and brought up massive anxiety and fear.

Belief

This meant my parent's being divorced was wrong and something was broken so, I took on the responsibility to fix it. I have always been tenacious, so believe me, I tried everything. I made cards; talked to them both until I was blue in the face, and wished on every birthday candle for years that my parents would get back together. When I ultimately (and obviously) failed, not only did I take on the belief that it must be my fault, but also that I was a failure for not being able to fix it. To compensate and therefore prove my worth, I began an exhausting pursuit to fix everything for everyone, which manifested into the ultimate people pleaser.

I remember a specific example of the class acting up one afternoon we had a substitute teacher. Having a full mental breakdown, I was sobbing and hyperventilating in the hallway out of the extreme fear of getting into trouble. I did the same thing on the school bus multiple times. I didn't want to cause trouble or displease anyone, especially adults. Deciding I would need to earn love and earn my right to exist, I needed to keep everything in line, making everything perfect, and control anyone and anything around me to feel safe, to be liked, to be approved of, and to make sure nothing else would break because of me. I became the greatest rule follower and helper you ever did see. At just six years old, I began silencing any opinion that would challenge authority and stepped into the best good-girl role I could play. I filled up my backpack with my first weights: **Excessive Over-Thinking, Fear, and People Pleasing Tendencies.**

Second Grade

Second grade was the most challenging year of my adolescence. It was full of massive life changes, realizations, and many of my traumatic, line-in-the-sand moments were compiled into one very overwhelming year.

#2 DAD'S MARRIAGE
AND THE BABIES

When my parents divorced, my mom met my stepdad relatively quickly and he fit right into my world. I didn't have alone time with my mom the way I did with my dad. My earliest memories, Jackson, my stepdad, lived with us. I call him Jack. He didn't have any kids and was so loving. Jack accepted me as his own from day one. Pushing me in the tire swing, teaching me how to play softball, and tucking me into bed at night, "wrapping me up like a burrito". Jack treated my older brother with the same love, and I have been immensely grateful for him throughout my life. He's one of the best people I know, and I remember my mom being so happy. I remember being happy for her as well. I don't remember feeling hurt or jealous over their relationship, besides wishing we all (my dad included) could live in the same house lol. There was this mindset I formed early on about being first to someone. Someone's number one priority. I always felt my mom had found her person, and he came first to her now.

My dad remained single for a few years, and I got comfortable in my time shared with him and my brother on Wednesdays and every other weekend. I felt like my dad's number one. My dad's first pick. The baby, the only girl, his girl. I can still hear the radio when he made breakfast on Saturdays and can still remember what the comforter felt like on his bed. Memories of the cold air when he would carry me at five am to take me back to my mom on his way to pour concrete, and the smell of coffee and sawdust in his truck. Riding the lawnmower on his lap and kneeling next to him and my brother at church every Sunday. I have vivid memories of him staying an extra ten minutes in my mom's driveway to talk to, and love on our dog that moved with us and mom after the divorce. He loved that dog.

I share the memories because I find it very telling those are the core memories I hold, and many of the memories following my dad remarrying are fuzzy and few. It tells me in my perception and the way I stored the memories, a piece of my world was gone when he met my stepmom.

When I met her, she was a major threat to my ego. She had two kids of her own, both close in age, and my relationship with her did not flow as naturally as that with my stepdad. In my eyes, she was someone taking my dad. Even though my relationship with my stepdad was easier, it did not make my childhood easy in either household. Both my parents and their spouses had their struggles, as we all do.

My Dad and my stepmom married, and she had back-to-back pregnancies bringing my two little brothers into the world, and I adored them. Now my every-other- weekend with my dad and older brother turned into a full, chaotic house. Two babies under two and a family of eight. A yours, mine, and ours dynamic full of beauty and so many challenges. My dad had a new first in my eyes.

At my moms, she and my stepdad also welcomed a new little brother. I loved the babies, and I felt as if I had disappeared into the sea of excitement and chaos.

Maybe this was middle-child syndrome, I'm not sure. What I know is the next belief I threw into my backpack was **Never First,** and I would begin an exhausting pursuit to find my person. A fairytale desire was born. I dreamt about finding my prince and getting married. For once I found my person, I would finally get my turn at being first.

#3 THE TEACHER

What do second graders learn about, anyway? A quick Google search led me to this answer for you:

> Developing and sustaining foundational language skills: listening, speaking, reading, writing, and thinking—self-sustained reading. The student reads grade-appropriate

texts independently. The student is expected to self-select text and interact independently with text for increasing periods of time.

To be anything of importance in the second grade, you needed to know how to read, and do you want to know what I struggled with? You guessed it, reading. To add to that, on a human emotional level, I would argue second graders have a whole other plethora of topics they are learning about. How to interact in new environments, how to make friends, how to handle and process emotions, how to balance responsibility as school gets more challenging, being able to juggle sports, friends, all while keeping their room clean. As well as what they like, how to express themselves, and how to handle whatever additional stress or pressure they are carrying from their home lives they may or may not speak about.

I struggled to make many friendships and felt on the outskirts of the surrounding kids. Plus, I played a role of teacher's pet per my fear, and I was bossy, other kids didn't like that. From a very young age, I always felt more comfortable with adults and would spend a lot of recesses questioning, and probably annoying the teacher on playground duty instead of playing tag with those my age. Because of my obvious distress, I started seeing the school counselor and felt like a freak when they would *not so discreetly* call me out of class for my session. I didn't feel I belonged, and I never felt as if I was anyone's favorite friend, feeding right into my *never first* narrative. I had friends that would be my best friend one day, then would have a new best friend and not talk to me the next; this was damaging to my self-confidence and created a lot of anxiety going to school unsure what to expect day to day. One friend in particular was up and down constantly.

I spent a lot of years attempting to win her over and be *her first*, only to be let down when she would choose someone else for a sleepover, take another girl on vacation, or when she would announce she had a new best friend for that week. The whole thing would destroy me inside. Always feeling everything so deeply, I was desperate for acceptance.

As I was navigating all the stress and life changes of my home life and school, I began having night terrors. If you've never heard of such a thing, I will enlighten you because they were, well, terrifying. I would go to sleep as normal and sleepwalk. Not only did I sleepwalk, but I would scream and cry as I was walking around in circles, leaving my parents feeling completely helpless because I was asleep, creepily, with my eyes open, having nightmares for months. The scariest part about them is I would have no recollection. I would wake up in the morning having no clue I scared the hell out of my mom and stepdad the night before. These continued for a very long time. I once walked by my mom, eyes open, unlocked the back door, and walked to the edge of the woods, asleep the entire time. When I started going to sleepovers, I had to warn my friends' parents of my possible attempt to escape.

Night terrors are a sleep disorder in which a person quickly awakens from sleep in a terrified state. The cause is unknown, but night terrors are often triggered by fever, lack of sleep or **periods of emotional tension, stress or conflict.**

With you filled in on the backstory of where I was emotionally as a seven-year-old, let me set the scene for my second-grade parent teacher conference. Do you remember yours? If I had to guess I would assume no, it's not typically something that makes the core memory bank for a child however, I'm sure you have your own version of a memory that would have typically been *just another day* that burned into your mind in significance forever.

The first thing I would like to note that I find interesting is the fact I was present for this conversation. This wasn't a memory I have from my mom telling me. I heard this straight from my teacher's mouth. The second thing I would like to note is this teacher never liked me. She was rude, cold, and I was always in trouble. None of my people pleasing tactics ever worked on her and I swear, she had it out for me.

I sat in a little plastic chair next to my mom when my teacher said bluntly; "She is far behind. She struggles with reading and comprehension. I'm afraid she will probably never read past a third-grade reading level and there is a strong possibility she will struggle academically for the rest of her career."

What did I hear? She is stupid and will always be stupid. She will never amount to anything in life. That would play on repeat in the back of my subconscious mind for years to come, like a broken record no one could shut off.

Little tears of anger and hurt welled up in my eyes.

It is absolutely mind blowing to me still twenty years later that a teacher would hex such a prophecy on an innocent little girl that obviously had so much she was struggling with.

"Struggle to function in society eternally" for a little trouble with a Judy Moody book is a bit dramatic, Miss G, don't you think? (I'm aware I'm also dramatic, but that is what it felt like.)

Belief

This experience could have gone one of two ways. I could have decided she was right. I could have believed I was stupid and chosen a life of mediocrity. Thankfully, I took from that conversation the alternative. "Watch me" was the energy. This response, however, still had its cost. I had already mastered being a "good girl," and the best rule follower/helper I could be. Now I would master achievement. Already being the class pet, now I would become the one singing the loudest, winning the art show, and the best at gym class. Yet another exhausting pursuit began, this time of being the best. I outworked everyone in any and every category. School, sports, beauty, humor. Another layer added to my desire to be chosen, to be first, desperately trying to prove my worth to anyone that would listen. Quite fascinating how we as humans develop survival mechanisms, one of which in my opinion being manipulation.

I became a master manipulator which feels dark to say, but looking back on my childhood, it is the truth. I was seven. There wasn't a conscious pursuit to manipulate with an evil laugh behind my bedroom door, it was about survival. I began studying people, studying human behavior, and learning how I could influence the people around me to agree with me. One way I figured out how to manipulate others was with my beauty. Being a beautiful little girl with long, curly hair and big brown eyes, I received a lot of attention. Some things have been much easier in my life because of physical beauty, and some, a lot harder. I was also very good with my words. Language has always been my thing. I learned how to make people laugh and to entertain them. The manipulating probably started much younger, however, it accelerated during this time out of a desperate desire to be loved. I think humans are born knowing how to manipulate and play on emotion. If you don't believe me, possibly you haven't had the experience of a toddler working you over with fake tears, a batting of the eyes, or a "pleaseeeee mommy?" If you aren't a parent, I'm sure you've experienced something similar from a sibling, niece or nephew, or hell, a dog or cat can manipulate you in a second given the chance to get another treat, or to go outside if they want to. It can show up in many forms and we grab on to whatever edge we have is my theory. Maybe we are the youngest, the smallest, the only girl. We use our beauty, humor, intelligence, an illness, or injury for an example to get what we want. I have a lot of theories on how this can manifest. However, for me, it mainly showed up in over-achieving perfectionism; doing anything I could for love and approval, and it far overstayed its welcome.

An additional weight added to the belief backpack; I could earn my worth through achievement. **Perfectionist/Over Achiever activated.**

#4 SCARED OF THE DARK

It was a Friday or Saturday night, and my mom and Jack were getting ready to go out. I'm not sure where they were going. Possibly on a date, to a friend's house, to the bar — I don't remember. However, what I know is my older brother was going to be babysitting me for the night. He was eight years older than me, so he must have been about fifteen or sixteen. Different babysitters would watch me from time to time, and I stayed home with my brother when I needed to if my mom was at work, or had to run somewhere, no biggie. I remember whining because I didn't want them to leave. I loved when they had friends over to our house because I got to be a part of it. I didn't like the thought of being left out of anything. My mom assured they wouldn't be home late, and I would be fine with my brother. I always got something fun if they went out like a lunch-able or a blockbuster movie and some popcorn -*woah blast from the past.*

They finished getting ready and left for the night. Shortly after they left, my brother came into the living room to announce that he was also leaving. His best friend lived on our street, a few houses down, and he told me he would be going there for a few hours. "If you tell mom, I'll kill you. Lock the door, you will be fine. I'll be back in a bit." Panic filled me as I argued he couldn't do that, and he was supposed to be watching me. He had made his mind up, and he was my big brother, so I wasn't going to argue, and I wasn't telling. He left, and I locked the door behind him. Terror ensued.

We lived in a modular surrounded by woods, and in the daylight, I spent tons of time alone and loved it. In the 90s and early 2000s we had a lot more freedom as kids. I would explore the woods or take off on my bike as long as I followed the rule everyone knew; Back by the time the streetlights turned on. I thrived in nature. My nickname when I was little was tootsie-roll because my skin would get so tan in the summers. I enjoyed my freedom, but not in the dark. Hating the dark, and fears of it lingered ever since this night. We had a second fridge in our garage where we stored all our sodas. I remember I would have to hype myself up well into my teenage years to sprint out the back door, down the stairs, across the deck, into the garage, grab my Orange Crush and sprint back praying whatever lived in the dark wouldn't get me, and that fear never really went away.

I spent the whole evening in a state of panic, running from room to room looking out all the windows, my mind running wild with all the scenarios of monsters or bad guys that were going to get me. I cried, and I jumped at every creek and sound. Balling up in a corner by the couch, I prayed for everyone to come home. I feel until this night I only saw the world as a magical place, and the fear I experienced took a piece of my innocence and inner child and held it there, frozen in a memory, until I would go back to retrieve her.

Belief

Trust issues entered the belief backpack. Trust issues with authority, with the feminine, and with the masculine, as I subconsciously blamed my mom and my brother for leaving me. More fear climbed in, and specifically more fear of being **alone.**

I recalled this memory during a session and worked through it with a coach using something called Neuro-Linguistic Programming, which is a pseudoscientific approach to communication, personal development, and psychotherapy. NLP tries to detect and modify unconscious biases or limitations of an individual's map of the world. *NLP is not hypnotherapy. Instead, it operates through the conscious use of language to bring about changes in someone's thoughts and behavior.*

She took me into a guided meditation to recall the first childhood memory where I felt fear, and this is what came up. I was reliving the memory through my eyes. I could see what everything in the house looked like that night. I could hear my mom's voice. I experienced all the anxiety in my chest all over again, and everything was in vivid color. Using the NLP, she walked me through a few exercises and then guided me back into meditation again. The second time I replayed the memory, everything was no longer in color, but in black and white. I watched the memory like a movie once more, but this time as an observer. I could no longer hear my mom's voice, or feel the anxiety in my chest, using these therapies allowed me to go back in time and heal a layer of pain that got stored in my subconscious mind.

Perspective

In today's world, having divorced parents is very common. By the time I graduated eighth grade, half my class had blended families. Today's first graders are more than likely very used to seeing every kind of family, however twenty years ago in my small town, in my catholic school, and in my seven-year-old brain I was different. I was an outlier; I was alone, my family was *broken*, and the worst belief I clung to is that somehow, my parents being divorced was *wrong*, and it was all my fault. I took on a weight I was never meant to carry, all based out of illusion. There was nothing wrong with my parents being divorced, especially if it created a healthier environment. My parents didn't "mess me up" by getting divorced. The reality is there was probably an equal to-or higher chance of "messing me up" if they were to force themselves to stay in a relationship, one or both were no longer happy in.

Another harsh reality is even though *my* memory and perception of having my dad all to myself was some of the best memories of my childhood, my dad spent a lot of time alone, and it was only a matter of time until he met someone, and he deserved to. This is where inner child work can get harry in our brains. It is not what happens in our lives that impact us most, it is the beliefs we form as a result. My dad was living his life. He didn't do anything wrong by dating, remarrying, and finding happiness. None of the pain I felt or emotions I went through were *his fault*. They were just a byproduct of how I perceived my world. My dad was young, attractive, and an amazing man. More than likely, he was going to meet someone when he was ready. Regardless of who that was going to be, she was going to be a threat in my little girl eyes. She was going to take my spot and push me into second best, I had already decided that long before I met her. I think that's often-times human nature, would you agree? The way a little boy feels protective over their mom, a little girl their dad, it's a special relationship when healthy, and even though it's totally justified a parent move on after divorce and love again, there is a death and grieving process for *the way things once were*.

In ALL families, things go on in different levels of severity. Regardless of the shape it took, chances are you have some childhood trauma. In some cases, like my parents remarrying and having babies, no one did anything "wrong." However, it affected me as if they did. In other cases, an authority figure or someone close to you did do something wrong, (which I also experienced in many occurrences,) and a very important lesson I've learned is regardless of what kind of trauma you have, it is yours, and it matters. I used to weigh mine out with people who had horrific childhoods and would use it as a reason to lessen the hard things I walked through, and I don't do that anymore.

"It could have been worse, at least I didn't go through that," or "at least I had one parent," for example. None of those, or any statements alike, serve. I own it, and I can acknowledge some things I went through were fucked up. I invite you to acknowledge, possibly for the first time, the things you experienced that hurt or scared you. Acknowledging times when you were hurt, scared, ignored, or felt insignificant for any reason are valid. I ask you to please not water down or dishonor your pain because someone else's was *"worse."* Awareness and acceptance are two of our strongest superpowers in our healing.

When it comes to blended families, it is one of the most difficult dynamics to face emotionally. Jealousy, different beliefs, and resentment are all a piece of the pie. I can make my point in this case without getting into all of it, we will save that tea for my relationships. I choose not to share the intimate details of my childhood out of respect for not telling my family's stories for them. I believe people do the best they know how to do and that's a belief I invite you to take on regarding any trauma, especially with your childhood.

We each have had our own life experiences and traumas that have shaped us, and what we don't heal unfortunately affects our children. It's a part of life. (Insert Simba being raised above the crowd with the *circle of life* soundtrack starting to fade in)

I believe in forgiveness.

Feeling the anger, sadness, or whatever emotion you have is equally important. I've found it serves me to take on a belief in understanding and empathy. However, being careful to not justify behavior because of it. One of my favorite quotes is "be kind, but not weak" *by Jim Rohn.*

What's pertinent to this story is how I *felt.* In my world, what was true for me, and my experience, was that of feeling very unwanted, disrespected, mistreated, less than, forgotten about, and even bullied during this period of my childhood. I spent a lot of time alone, was very anxious at school, and I lived in a heightened sense of fear, like I mentioned.

I also experienced so much joy, creativity, love, and feelings of safety. My childhood was full of duality. Many of our experiences are overlooked or misrepresented in a culture that only highlights extremes. My childhood wasn't a princess dreamland, and it also wasn't a horrific nightmare.

Being a human IS duality. My childhood was amazing, *and* very lonely and very painful. All parts are true and necessary, and one lesson reflecting on this season of my life is to release the social programming around shadows, and hiding a reality so many of us can relate too. The 90s, early 2000s, and unfortunately still today a *white picket fence, keeping up with the Joneses* culture remains, and it must go. Being a human is amazing, beautiful, painful, and MESSY!

For me, finding peace means acknowledging that our parents did their best, even if it wasn't always enough.

To add perspective to my teacher and the role she played in my world, it's quite simple, really. Some things there aren't answers for, and we get to learn to be okay with that. Not everyone has the same heart. Her words were not empowering, and most would agree unfair, however life can be unfair sometimes. I will never know why she disliked me the way she did, or maybe in her world she didn't feel that way at all, and she was just a very direct person.

The point is, it doesn't matter. Something I had to overcome was believing I could make everything make sense. Some things you went through will never make sense. All I know is she did her job. She triggered something that lead me down a path of lessons to be learned, and one lesson I learned here, is someone's opinion of you, or vision they have for your life does not have to become your reality. When I typed that, I heard Les Brown's voice in my head, so shout out Les!

"Someone's opinion of you does not have to become your reality,"
– Les Brown

Lastly, for my night with the darkness. Are my mom and stepdad negligent parents for having a social life after having kids? Up for interpretation, I suppose, however I say absolutely not. Of course not, and my brother loves me. He shouldn't burn in hell for doing a stupid, very common, big brother teenager thing.

Healing

I heard an amazing quote once that really supported in my healing.

"Holding on to bitterness or resentment is like drinking
poison and expecting the other person to die."
— Malachy McCourt

YOU are the one that carries the negative energy, the pain, the anger; you are the one drinking the poison. What I found empowering about that is if I am the one with the power here, I also have the choice to stop drinking the poison. To truly forgive, and to look at life through a lens of empathy. That *everyone* is doing the best they know how to do. Some people do unexplainable, horrible things and I am in no way justifying that. I am however offering a perspective that feels empowering because we have no control over what anyone did or said, or the way we were treated, and possibly look through a lens of the painful experiences we've faced serving us, preparing us, and teaching us feels better than drowning in a victim mentality. I'm offering a perspective of our experiences giving us a three-dimensional life school for our soul to develop, heal, and grow.

"We do not see the world as it is, we see the world as we are." -Anais Nin is where I found the original quote but heard it first years ago from *Rachel Hollis*.

This perspective is one that will follow every lesson and chapter in this book.

The more time we take to become aware of who we are, how we see the world, and put in the work to grow and learn from these experiences, we take our power back, we transition out of victimhood, and become our own savior.

What if my parent's divorce was aligning the exact family dynamic and challenges I needed to face and overcome to prepare and equip me for my destiny?

What if the friend that never chose me played an integral role in my learning independence?

What if that night in the darkness needed to happen, so I could later learn to face fear and rise?

What if I was gifted that teacher to light a fire within me to become something big in life?

> *"What happens to us is not our fault, however,*
> *is our responsibility to heal it,"*
> – Will Smith

I'm a natural born debater, so for the sake of the argument, let's look at both sides of this belief. Most would agree to anything that happened to you as a child that hurt you, scared you, or traumatized you wouldn't be your fault. However, many, my past self-included, may have a difficult time aligning with taking responsibility for their own healing, and I can understand that thought, especially if you were a victim. As a child, you're in your purest, most innocent form and any mistreatments from anyone, whether parents, teachers, friends at school, siblings, whoever, are unjust, and feeling victimized, is valid. However, living in a victim mentality will never allow you freedom.

I am not sure what you've been through. I'm unsure how severe, however, I believe we all have only one choice to gain freedom. Feel the pain, feel the anger, and let it go. Carrying our past around on our back begins to break down not only our back, but our spirit. Taking responsibility for your healing journey gives you power, gives you peace. The strength to say "what happened to me was not my fault, I didn't deserve it, **and** I made the choice to heal; to forgive anyway. I made the choice to take my power back, to love my scars, and to end a curse and a way of being; a way of thinking and behaving that possibly has gone on for generations."

"*It runs in the family*" is a saying often used, whatever resonates with you. Maybe lack mentality, poverty, alcoholism, lack of self-worth, abuse of any kind, suppression of emotion, addictions, people pleasing, whatever has *"run in the family"* you can decide that here, this is where it runs out: with you.

Another empowering reason I believe healing is our responsibility is a huge premise for this book. If not you, then who? Who is going to come in to save the day and help you change your life? There's a Mel Robbins motivational video where she says, *"no one is coming."* There is a very good chance people have hurt you and you will never get an apology. After reading this book and choosing to do your own work, I believe you'll be able to move on and thrive peacefully without one. If you fall into the trap of allowing someone else to be your savior or to validate you, you will head down a rough road of codependency. Trust me, I took that path first. You're about to read all about it lol.

If you're reading this, I invite you to take a big deep breath in. Exhale slowly and find peace and power within to know that even if it's scary, and no matter how long the road, you have now found a resource to guide you to being your own hero.

Weights accumulated in my belief backpack:

Excessive Overthinking
Fear
People Pleasing
A "Never First" Mentality
Over Achiever
Perfectionism
Trust Issues
Codependency
I Need Saved

This next section of the book will begin my journey in love. Let's see how these beliefs I was carrying showed up in relationships.

CHAPTER TWO

PUPPY LOVE

I had my first kiss the summer before my eighth-grade year. It fully fulfilled my fairy tale dreams as it was pouring down rain and felt like a Taylor Swift serenaded music video. Yes, I am dramatic. I have always been dramatic, and my life is, has always been, and will always be a movie. It's something I've manifested and attracted since birth. I feel everything so deeply as I've shared and see my life as an incredible movie with one plot twist after another. *The Notebook* love scenes, *Kevin Hart* quality comedy and *Fast and the Furious* drama, action, and thrills.

This is my first boyfriend; we will call him Luke. My first innocent puppy love. He was two years older than me, and I thought he was the most adorable, coolest person on the planet. He was my best friend's older cousin, so I saw him around often, and always had the biggest crush on him. There was always teasing from my friend and her parents because we were both so cute and flirtatious. He had my whole fourteen-year-old heart wrapped up.

This was the start of a pattern I would fall into for years, never having any understanding of the disconnect, and why I loved so hard and so quickly. We now know I was carrying my heavy belief backpack, and this was the point of my life where my focus shifted. I went from a girl looking for validation from parents and teachers, to peers and love interests. So began my wide-eyed, naïve view of love and over-trust in people and their intentions. I was looking for my person, and the desire was deeply rooted in all the weight of my childhood.

Luke was very innocent, kind, and I truly believed he felt about me the way I did him, however he was a sixteen-year-old boy lol. I watched him change and lose his innocence going into high school, which I now understand was totally normal. Look, realistically I shouldn't have even been dating someone that much older than me because two years isn't a lot, however the changes between fourteen to sixteen are paramount. I was in the "hold hands and cuddle" phase with a few make out sessions sprinkled in before being home by my curfew. He was ready to move past that stage and cheated on me with a cheerleader. I was crushed.

Now let's not spend our time demonizing a hormone- raging sixteen-year-old boy and focus on the incident and what I made it mean: I was cheated on by my first boyfriend. The first masculine energy I trusted and had feelings for betrayed me, and my first experience dating ended in heartbreak and feelings of loss. This was also my first experience of attachment. I put my full focus and happiness into this boy. The sun rose and set with him. This was a weight Luke never asked for, and a weight he couldn't carry, setting me up for teenage devastation when he was gone.

Lessons

There are a few paths I could have taken in this scenario, like the experience with the teacher. We always have a choice. One choice would be to go cold; to lose trust in others, become skeptical of love, and completely shut down, allowing my first experience of rejection as proof of all the negative beliefs I held true. I could have stopped myself from sharing my heart again to protect it, and many take that path. Another path could have been learning from the experience. With a chip on my shoulder, I could have slowed down the next time I liked someone. I could have learned from this first experience that not everyone has the same heart or intentions and I needed to allow space in relationships for my partner to earn the respect and access to my heart I so freely gave. However, I chose neither of those. I felt deep levels of pain, fed my negative beliefs superfood, and went back again.

My greatest gift and sometimes my biggest challenge is my heart. I love deeply, widely, and again and again regardless of what happens. The best visual for my dating life I can share is that of a puppy that never stops running to greet an owner. I always saw light in everyone, and time and time again used that light as an excuse to accept their darkness. I went back and forth with this puppy love many times, and it was only foreshadowing how I would operate in every relationship. I was notorious for second chances, or let's be real, fifth chances in relationships, never holding it against my partner. I would grant them the same source of love, trust, and respect, usually by words they promised me, as I would be blind to their actions.

Unconditional love is the most natural concept to me and always has been. The beauty of unconditional love is undeniable, yet I overlooked a crucial lesson.

Unconditional love does *not* equal unconditional tolerance.

My ability to forgive made me a doormat and a target for anyone looking to manipulate others because I always offered compassion, no matter what treatment I faced. It wasn't an inability to speak up. Forgiveness comes naturally to me. The boundary I needed to learn was forgiving, but not forgetting. Basing my decisions on the light and the potential I saw in others was where I was going wrong. Basing my decisions off words, not actions. True unconditional love starts with deep love and respect for self, which comes before all other outside parties. Unconditional love of self means seeing a situation for what it is and not for what it *could be*.

A Pattern

I took everything personally. My inner six-year-old controlling my now adolescent life feeling *wrong, bad, and in trouble*. Similar to when I made decisions about my parent's divorce, I now decided with this first heartbreak it was my fault, and I wasn't good enough. The **reality** was I was in an early relationship with a teenage boy and his actions had nothing to do with me. SAY IT AGAIN FOR THE PEOPLE IN THE BACK. Most of the time, another person's actions HAVE NOTHING TO DO WITH YOU. Have nothing to do with you, your worth, or your value. I was so hungry for love and approval; I became blind. I took words as sacred truth because to me they are, and always have been. A child is hopeful, and often naïve, I was operating from this place emotionally setting me up for a rough road.

If I could have a conversation with my sweet young self, I would do my very best to explain these lessons before she spent the next ten years learning them repeatedly in harsher and harsher ways. I would say,

"Nothing you could do, be, or achieve could make you *enough* for the wrong person. How someone else perceives you is out of your control and therefore deserves freedom from your mind. Your worth in this world is not reliant on how a boy, or later a man, treats you. You're perfect as you are and anyone you allow into your life should treat the opportunity as a privilege. If you're crying more than you're happy, he isn't a fit partner. If you feel insecure, unsure, or unsafe, remove yourself from the relationship. Boundaries are your birthright. You do not owe anyone an answer, a reason, or access to you at all if they are hurting you or disturbing your peace. You can, and should say NO. Head up beautiful, let them lose you, and thank them for showing you what you do, and do not want in partnership. Please, enjoy being fifteen and stop taking life so seriously. Embrace how deeply you feel, but remember to be in each experience and understand nothing is permanent. You can't mess anything meant for you up, and you have a lot of time."

Trigger warning of sexual trauma and suicide in the following chapter.

CHAPTER THREE

TRAUMA BOND

The first time I saw him was at a city park blacktop. It was a warm summer night with a slight chill filling the air as the sun went down. He was playing a game of pickup basketball with a bunch of guys.

He had a cutoff shirt on, shorts, and a pair of Jordans as he jumped up and dunked the ball, laughing and shouting on the way down; a core memory for me.

"Who is that?" I asked one of the girls I was there with.

"That's Adam" Miranda said. The name she said quickly sobered me, as I was now aware this was the boy we were here for Riley to see. *Her* boy. Riley I was learning was the queen bee, and every cute or popular guy from any school had a thing for her. It was a bit wild to see the hold she had over them all. I was excessively loyal, and I admired her. I also didn't think Adam would ever pay attention to me anyway, so I let the heart beating fast subside and stayed in my place: quiet.

Miranda and Riley were the two girls I had been hanging around with. They were in Luke's grade, so again, two years and a world of experience older than me. Eager to be corrupted, I was their cute, innocent, little Catholic schoolgirl tagalong. I experienced a lot of firsts with these two: first time lying to my parents, first time going to a party, first time shot gunning a beer. During a spin the bottle game at Riley's house, I remember her saying, "If it lands on Penelope, you have to give her a hug." Playing the role of a good girl because I wanted the approval of adults had shifted. Now I was seeking the approval of "cool kids" and boys, so my approach had to shift as well. This was the beginning of my time of rebellion.

I had major guilt and anxiety with every decision because, although the desire to be accepted trumped the desire to please authority figures, that belief backpack still weighed heavily. I remember the extreme fear I had lying to my mom saying I was sleeping over down the street when really, I was an hour away at some house party with people I didn't even know, and often would be left at some point in the night when Riley, Miranda, or both would disappear with a guy. I would hardly drink out of fear in the beginning and would sleep with Riley's car key lanyard around my neck to guarantee she wouldn't lose them and could get me home in time to make it to church the next day like she promised.

My phone rang the first night I was at a house party as my worst fear came to life, my mother calling at 11:30PM. "She knows," I panicked. I yelled for Riley to save me as we locked ourselves in a closet to answer the phone. "Play it cool," she ordered. "Hello," I answered the phone, my voice shaking.

"PENELOPE!" my mom yelled through the phone. My heart sank as I began mentally planning my funeral.

"SOMEONE TOILET PAPERED OUR HOUSE!" she yelled, Riley and I grabbing our chest with relief. I stumbled around the conversation as she laughed and told me we would be cleaning it up because it must have been my friends. Riley grabbed the phone, and more fear ran through my body as she had already been drinking. She turned on her charm, wrapping up the call assuring my mom we were about to watch a movie. We said I love you as she hung up. I was stunned, and we both screamed and celebrated, jumping around in the closet. She was a liar, and now so was I, but she was my hero lol.

There was one night a few months later we were back at the same house. I was sleeping on a couch when some guy climbed behind me. He thought I was asleep, but I wasn't. He slid the blankets, trying not to wake me as he ran his hands up my legs, trying to fit his hands up my shorts. I froze. I wanted to get up but couldn't get my body to move.

He stuck his hand up through my legs and just as I felt his fingers break past my underwear; I threw the blankets, jumped up and ran into the other room. Thankfully, he was passive, and it stopped there. I went into another room, my heart racing, and sat curled up without a blanket, knowing any kind of sleep was out of the question, waiting for Riley so we could leave. He pretended nothing ever happened and was sleeping on that same couch when I left. I never talked about it to anyone, and I am so thankful I got up, and that he allowed me to before anything else happened. Every time I saw him in the future, it made me feel sick to my stomach and added a layer of fear with men for me.

Everyone was standing around talking after the blacktop game ended. Feeling a chill, I went in search of warmth. I was incredibly shy and by far the youngest. Waiting in the car was fine with me.

"Are you cold or something?" He smiled as he popped his head into the driver's side window. Adam had the most piercing blue eyes and coal black hair. I had a hard time forming words to answer him.

"Yeah," I forced out.

"I have a sweatshirt if you want it. Are you coming to the party later? It will be fun. What is your name? I haven't seen you before."

"Uhm, I'm not sure, whatever they're doing, and Penelope."

"Penelope, wow." He smiled and left the car to go back to everyone outside, while I tried to remember how to breathe.

We went to the party, and I awkwardly shoved away anyone attempting to talk to me. My friends were wild, and there was a part of me that wanted to experience their freedom, but wasn't comfortable enough yet to jump all the way in.

I found myself a chair near a bonfire where I could safely be left alone while Miranda called to me to come play beer pong or flip cup. This was shortly after the party with the creep incident, and I was still on high alert of anyone around me or drinking too much around strangers.

(*I laugh typing this because I'm discussing being responsibly cautious of drinking too much when I was fifteen years old and illegally drinking in the first place, bless.*)

"I'm okay. You guys have fun!" I yelled back to Miranda.

Riley played this confusing game with boys I didn't understand. She would flirt with them, be very sweet to them, they would fall in love with her, then she would ignore them and play constant mind games. I watched her do it all the time, just observing and never asking questions. Well, this night, she shunned blue eyes. I don't know if she was drunk or mad at him or what, but at some point, the group all went into the house, and I saw him walking towards me at the fire. "Oh no," I thought. I wanted to disappear.

"Can I sit here?" he asked. I glanced at the door, worried about upsetting Riley. However, I was positive I wouldn't let anything happen.

"Sure," I said.

We talked for hours. Questions and back and forth across the fire. I was mesmerized by him, and committed to my integrity so I kept it innocent, and let's be real, I was innocent. Adam was nineteen, but I didn't feel the age difference. He was gentle and kind and wasn't insinuating any alterative motives.

The night got longer and longer until the sun was starting to come up and I was far past exhaustion. We went inside to find everyone asleep in random places and he said, "You can sleep in my room if you'd like, I won't touch you I swear," he laughed. There was no way in hell I was letting that happen, so I kindly declined and curled up on a chair two feet away from my friends. He stared at me before he went into his room, "goodnight, Penelope" he said, and I felt the loss of sleep every bit of worth it.

Riley didn't say a single word to me on the way home, Miranda in the front seat awkwardly finding herself in the middle of the tension. I tried to ask questions, grasping at approval that I wasn't in "trouble" because I feared her, and I knew I didn't do anything wrong. I can remember the anxiety and panic in my chest: someone not being happy with me was enough to derail me subconsciously reacting from my inner child. Riley's silence was her way of letting me know she was pissed.

They dropped me off at home and I awkwardly said, "see you guys," getting out of the car holding back tears. The rest of the day my mind wouldn't rest trying to find a way to make everything okay again: people pleaser lights flashing all around me.

"It was so nice to meet you. I can't stop thinking about last night," the text from Adam read. Not sure how he got my number, but I did know all I wanted to do was respond, but I didn't. Loyalty, remember?

That night was the church festival, everyone always went. Being from a small town, whenever something was happening, everyone would be there. A church parking lot filled with raffle baskets, homemade noodles, kids getting their face's painted, and a live band was the highlight of most of my summers.

I saw Miranda coming towards me from a food stand. "Penelope! Come with me. I need to talk to you."

I followed her to the bathroom hoping she would help me with my current mental warfare, telling me everything would be alright.

"What did she say to you!?" I demanded as soon as we were alone.

"It's not good," she said with a face, letting me down. "Riley said she's done with you, and you're just a little whore. She talked about you the entire way home."

I was crushed. I was angry, I was confused, and mainly felt betrayed because I realized this "friend" I was hellbent on protecting was so quick to throw me away without a second thought. (A hard lesson each of us learns at some point, I believe.) When you're a teenager, these things feel a much bigger deal than you realize they are, in retrospect. This felt like the end of the world.

"I didn't do anything!" I argued, "look I didn't even respond to his text message today," showing her my phone as proof.

I'll never forget Miranda closing the stall of the church community center bathroom and dramatically throwing her hands up, saying: "Well I say if she's going to call you a whore you might as well be one, we are going back there tonight!"

To be clear, she was using the term "whore" very loosely, as I was still very much a virgin and this was the worst advice ever; however, she was a wild child, and this advice led to some amazing *you are only young and dumb once* memories that I will cherish forever lol.

We went back that night and so began a four-year-long journey.

This moment was the birth of a two-year-long best friend relationship, and partner in crime alliance of complete recklessness, and some of the best memories of my adolescence. One memory that still sends me hysterically laughing was our car accident. We went to a party with Adam and his friends and stayed the night there. Miranda and I got up at seven in the morning to make it home without our parents questioning where we were. I don't remember, but I assume we both said we were at the other one's house. She drove, and I fell asleep. Well, apparently, so did she, and I woke up to the car flying into a ditch, slamming into the muddy bank, stopping us from rolling down a hill. We screamed, looked at each other to make sure we both were still alive, then masterminded how we were possibly getting out of that one. Our story was solid. No one would question us, we were sure of it. What was the well-crafted story, you ask? Why were we driving thirty minutes away at seven in the morning on a Sunday? We were delivering water. We were delivering water to Miranda's grandmother.

How on earth my mom believed this, or why she pretended to, is beyond me. I came home with black feet from a bonfire, a large boys' basketball t-shirt on, and our story was a wholesome water delivery to the elderly.

Love

I've spent a lot of time pondering the dynamic of a first love. What about them makes them so intense and burned into our memory? I mean, I can replay every part of the scene I just shared and much of the four years following vividly. One theory I have is it may have not even been the person specifically, but the anticipation and idolization leading up to the relationship. Movies, love songs, and fantasies from childhood about being in love. I think it sends a lot of us into this high expectation of the first time we experience feelings, this is going to be *the one* and as we know in my case, I had a concrete belief that once I found *the one* my inner pain would finally subside. All my problems would fade away. I would find my hero, finally be first, and live life happily ever after.

Innocence

We were inseparable from that night on as much as we could be. Any chance I got to get out of my house, I was going to see him. Our adoration for each other was equal. He showed complete respect for all my boundaries and communicated his love through written letters, songs, and text messages. While I was at practice, he left presents in my car and made homemade cards for me frequently. We spent any night I could sneak out at a bonfire party or sitting at the park.

Then my mom found out.

She asked to use my phone for something, and I remember the panic setting in as I tried to remain calm, she would just use it quickly and give it back. She did not. I saw her face start to change as I realized she was reading my text messages. I was begging her for the phone back, having a full mental breakdown, but she refused. "Who is Adam?" She demanded. I refused to tell her.

She threatened me with not giving my phone back and said that she would find out anyway, so I might as well tell her.

I told her his name and that he was my boyfriend; then began the interrogation. When she found out how old he was, she ripped my heart out of my chest without skipping a beat.

"ABSOLUTELY NOT!" she yelled. "You are not to see him again Penelope, he's nineteen-years old. NO way in hell!"

The tears were immediate, and I begged her to listen. "You don't understand. I love him!" She wasn't hearing it, waving away my drama with her hand. I spent the rest of the day sobbing uncontrollably, feeling waves of sadness and rage.

There's always been something innate in me when I truly want something. My desire for it will not rest. As I grew out of my fearful inner child, I came into a strong dislike of authority and rules. All this to say, nothing or no one was stopping me from seeing him. I spent the next few months sneaking around and lying, Romeo and Juliet style.

Adam called one day to announce he was coming to my house to talk to my mom, and he asked me to prepare her. I was against it for fear I would be grounded for life; however, he was confident it would work. His sincerity and love were apparent to me because he never pressured me physically, and we had been together for five months. Do you know many nineteen-year-old boys? For a nineteen-year-old to fight to be with me, a girl three years younger, without sex being a factor; in my eyes, it must have been love.

He came to my house dressed up and brought my mom flowers, asking for her permission to date me, under whatever circumstances she would agree to. No way in hell I was involving my dad because I was positive he would have killed him and that would have been the end of that lol. She caved. He was very convincing, and very charming. Jack protested but always respected my mom's final say.

Her contingencies at first were him coming to our house, certain curfews, and things of that nature. However, the longer time went on, the boundaries softened, and he became a part of our family, and I made my way right into his.

Adam had the best family and the sweetest mother on the face of the planet. When I first met his parents, I could feel the obvious reservation and probably confusion as to why he was dating someone so much younger, but after meeting me and seeing us together, they understood. His mom grew to love me, and I really loved her. They were very religious and so giving to their community; I looked up to the way his parents loved each other and how his mom made an amazing dinner every night. She would hug me every time I came over and so intently would ask me how my day was or if she could get me anything. I loved being at his house.

On his birthday, I surprised him with homemade cupcakes. The joy on his face when I woke him up from a nap jumping on top of him fills my mind as I recall the memory and I can still feel the way I felt protected when he wrapped me up in a hug. He towered over me, making me feel tiny. There are a lot of sweet memories like this one in the first year. I remember going to the Christmas lights at the zoo and watching him nervously getting the jewelry bag out of his coat pocket to give me the Zale's necklace he got me for Christmas. I was the happiest I had ever been, and he was beaming with pride to give it to me. "My mom helped me pick it out. Do you like it?" He asked.

I loved it, and I never took it off. I found myself in a fairy tale, completely oblivious to anything that could disrupt it.

I lost my virginity on New Year's Eve. I was sixteen and I remember being surprised when I didn't feel shame. My family was Catholic, and I was feared into believing I would be damned to a fiery hell if I had sex before marriage. I always thought I would wait. However, I never aligned with the "damned to hell" narrative. I was always highly romantic and felt as if I had been born into the wrong era. I didn't feel shame. It felt just right, and I was grateful to share it with someone I loved deeply. Of course, I thought I would marry that kid, so that also was a factor in my reasoning.

That level of connection only deepened my feelings, and for a few more months, our loving relationship continued.

Things Changed

Eventually, the honeymoon phase faded, and we began to argue. I was a volatile teenager at this point and some of my attitude was unwarranted.

Adam, on the other hand, started being very possessive and controlling. He started to isolate me from other people. I was in high school. I played sports; I had friends. I gradually attended Friday night football games and school dances less and less to spend time with him. What I wasn't realizing was I was missing a huge part of my adolescence, and looking back, I feel that was intentional because I never felt I belonged. I dealt with a few groups of mean girls over the years, and I found it easier just to separate myself. Regret is not something I carry; however, it has often crossed my mind what it would have been like to date a football player and wear his jersey. To be my age instead of hitting fast forward through every season. When I was in middle school, I was partying with high schoolers, when I was in high school, I was missing out on life to be an adult. He didn't like me being anywhere without him.

The thing about abusive relationships is if we are honest, we can pinpoint gut feelings or red flags when they began, however we often ignore them until they escalate to a dangerous place. His subtle comments about any of my male friends, or minor forms of manipulation to get me to stay home from a game or school dance afterparty were some beginning signs. Also, his language started to change. The first day he called me a name should have been enough of a sign. Once that line was crossed, it was only a matter of time until it would be the norm whenever he was angry. "Stupid bitch," he would say as I would slam the car door in tears, trying to get away from him. Only for him to jump out of the car to pick me up apologizing profusely with, "I'm sorry baby, I love you."

This toxic manipulation mind game started to deteriorate my confidence, my sense of safety, and my sanity.

He tore me down piece by piece with abuse, followed by toxic codependent "love."

I didn't notice a massive shift; it was like a current dragging you out to a point where you look up and don't know how you got a mile down the beach. He started partying, drinking heavily, and I didn't know this or understand then. However, he had started doing drugs. I found myself with this person I didn't recognize except in small glimpses.

What I understand now is the whole first year of our relationship was something called love bombing. *Love bombing is a form of psychological abuse that involves a person going above and beyond for you in an effort to manipulate you into a relationship with them. It looks different for every person, but it usually involves some form of: Excessive flattery and praise.*

There are so many painful stories and cycles of the next few years. From an outside perspective, it's hard to understand why anyone would stay with their abuser. People posing this question, I would guess, have never found themselves in the chokehold of a narcissist. I wish I could go back and hold that version of myself. I never told my parents or really anyone what went on. Abuse victims often not only remain with their abuser but also defend them. I'll share a few of the stories for context.

Darkness

Adam was partying a lot, and I got bits and pieces of the truth. I chilled out on the partying because I fell in love with basketball and had a couple of coaches that really changed my life, believed in me, and inspired me to a point of believing in myself and working hard for something. I started to be pulled down a path of success while simultaneously holding on to this toxic relationship with someone on a much different path. He was getting in trouble, getting kicked out of his house, constantly in between jobs, and I was practicing at five in the morning and trying to stay on the Honor Roll.

He cheated on me and lied all the time. He maintained strong control over my actions while doing whatever he pleased.

Everything he did, I was accused of. Narcissists are known to do this as well. If they are cheating, they will check your phone and question everything you do because they are projecting on to you.

I always felt wrong. I lived in fear, and I tiptoed on eggshells in every area of my life. He was triggering and tapping into every single one of my inner child's beliefs and only making them stronger. I blocked any male species from every form of contact, lost friends, and made calculated decisions in hopes of not making him mad.

He had gotten in trouble for something and wasn't able to go to this country concert we had planned to go to together. I thought I wouldn't be "allowed" and assumed I couldn't go anymore. Writing this makes me cringe, as the person I am now can't imagine living like this. However, I recognize that enduring this reality has given me strength to share my story. I digress.

I went over to his place, and he questioned whether I was looking forward to the concert, causing me to hesitate in fear of giving the wrong response. "Oh, I'm not going without you!"

"You have to," he said. "You shouldn't be punished just because I can't go. I want you to," Adam said with a smile.

Manipulation of the mind is a dark and scary thing in this kind of dynamic. There is never any safety or sense of reality because you have a foundation solidified in your mind of when they were nothing but loving. That reality now plays tricks on you because you find yourself in a constant heightened emotional state, never knowing what you're going to get. They aren't mean all the time or they wouldn't be able to keep or control you. This was an example of that. He was being logical; it wasn't fair for me to miss the concert because he couldn't go, and in a healthy relationship this would make sense. So, I went.

This concert was a defining moment in my memory because it shows the damage mentally that had been done. I didn't enjoy one second of the concert and spent most of it trying to get service to text him. I remember strategically moving my body to make sure I remained four-to six-feet away from any other guy.

I was so paranoid someone would take a picture of me, or he had someone watching me like this was a test I needed to pass.

"Penelope!" I heard a voice yell, realizing it was his best friend, Zach. I felt relieved to see him, almost as if he could be my alibi that I "behaved." "Let's call Adam," Zach said. In my perspective, showing him I was with his close friend would show him I was safe. In his demented head it meant I was- in his words, "fucking all his friends." Let's just say the phone call didn't go well, and I spent the rest of the night crying and being sick to my stomach. This was a repeated scenario. If I ever chose to do anything or go anywhere without him, he would make sure to ruin it.

Adam texted me the next morning with one of his apologies. It was always because he "loved me so much" and he was sorry for being upset. He "knew I would never do anything to hurt him," and begged me to come over to once again, make everything okay. I was living in a complete fog and always went back, accepting his apologies time after time. My memories of the past and my fantasies of the future anchored me into staying in the relationship because I had already decided he was *the one*. I was holding on to the version of himself he pretended to be the first year, refusing to accept the current reality.

I walked into his room, happy to see him after the long text messages I had received, and he stared at me with empty eyes and complete hatred.

"What are you doing here?" he retorted. I could barely utter words from complete confusion. He had just invited me over forty-five minutes before.

"What are you talking about?" I said sheepishly.

"Get the fuck out of here. I never want to see your face again," Adam said coldly. I felt the tears well up as I stood there, frozen. "You just.."

"Shut up!" He yelled, cutting me off.

"You think I meant any of that? After you went and whored around the entire night with my friends, you think I want anything to do with you? Get the fuck out of here!" He yelled, rolling over like nothing ever happened.

"Adam, I.." I stuttered, tears rolling down my face.

"GET OUT!" He screamed, shaking my nervous system to its core.

The overwhelming emotion turned into a full-blown panic attack by the time I rounded the corner to come down the stairs. I tried to get by his mom as quickly as possible through the kitchen. She followed me out to the driveway chasing me down and grabbed my shoulders with tears in her eyes and said, "listen to me!" I tried to stifle my tears and did as she said. "Do not come back, Penelope, please. Stay away from him. I don't recognize my son and I have to deal with him, but you don't! You are too sweet of a girl to be put through this, so please, I know it's hard, but."

The sound of Adam's bedroom window opening startled us both. "I SAID FUCKING LEAVE!" he screamed; his mom stared at him in disgust. Her eyes locked on mine one more time as if to tell me once more, or better yet to beg me "go."

I wish I could tell you that was the last time I saw him, but it wasn't, and things got progressively worse.

"I hope he rapes you."

He said coldly as he pointed to the homeless man on the side of the road. Adam had pulled the car over on a busy street corner, forcing me to get out, telling me he was going to leave me there after yet another fight.

I clutched on to my seatbelt, crying, begging him to stop, declaring that I wouldn't be getting out of the car. He continued yelling at me, trying to force my hands off the seatbelt. I fought long enough that he sped up the car with me still in it. His words shook me with fear and left me traumatized. I was still trying to wrap my head around them while texting Miranda's mom as fast as I could knowing she would come and get me. He slammed the car into park at the softball field and threw open his door mumbling angrily and left me standing there as he went towards the ball field. I sobbed there waiting at the furthest park bench I could find waiting on my ride while he went to play his game, smiling and laughing with his friends unphased. *"I hope he rapes you,"* rings so painfully in my ears as I write this. This wasn't my worst enemy, this was my partner. Someone who told me he loved me every day. Someone who really didn't care if I lived or died and would have slept fine knowing he dropped me off on the side of the road, wishing someone would have raped me.

Adam would charm my family, come to my basketball games, take me to church or sit with me and his family watching Sunday football and then scream in my face at a party or grab my wrists so tightly I would later have to heal post-traumatic stress from anyone touching me there. He threw me around but never hit me. I think it was because I never instigated or retaliated against him once he reached this point. Unfortunately, it probably would have escalated to that eventually if I would have stayed much longer. I'm not a fan of exploring that mental road.

Another level of mental manipulation he put me through was threatening suicide. Any time I tried to leave or break up with him he would send me messages telling me he how he would do it, and that it would be all my fault. He would call me crying at two in the morning, saying he was about to do it and hang up, not answering for hours. I remember sobbing, screaming, and being terrified he would go through with it, and I believed him when he said it would be my fault. I would go looking for him in the middle of the night or spend hours having panic attacks until I heard from him again. I remember one specific phone call one late night when he was drunk. He told me he was going to shoot himself in my front yard so I would have to see it, and he hoped I hated myself for leaving him.

He cheated on me more times than I could count and when I was eighteen got someone else pregnant. This was soul crushing then, and now feels like a gift from God.

I remember in the beginning getting a few threats from her, and then they both vanished. For about a year, he disappeared from my life completely. He got rid of social media and I heard he married her. In a logical world I should've been thrilled and set free. However, that is not how trauma, abuse, or trauma bonds work. I was devastated.

I eventually started to heal. I started to see friends again, go to school bonfires, and enjoyed my senior year for a bit. I met someone else a few months later as I clearly had a fear of being alone, and I dated him the remainder of the year.

A Blur

His name was Mason. This relationship was like a beacon of hope after a long period of darkness. He was one of the most selfless people I ever met. Me, him, and his best friend Andrea got a house together. (Yes, I moved out of my house while I was in high school.) Andrea had coached me in volleyball the year prior, and she was amazing. I had a lot of fun in that house playing "grown up." Yet again, he was entirely too old for me. I was eighteen and Mason was twenty- seven. Honestly, I was numb, and don't remember much of that year. What I know is the light-hearted, good people Mason and Andrea were restored some joy back into my dark world and I loved them. I tore my ACL that year ending my basketball career and was so low emotionally. I was in a relationship with Mason. However, the three of us created a sort of family dynamic friendship that I really needed. Although I cared for him, I knew he wasn't my future despite his feelings for me. Once I started to come out of my fog of survival mode, I realized I didn't want to be with him anymore. It was also apparent that he felt we were getting serious, and I was terrified of hurting him. A few weeks into battling this knowing I received a message that stopped my world on a dime.

It was a long Facebook message from Adam apologizing and asking to talk to me. I had every emotion you could imagine. Fear, relief, excitement, panic. While devastated at the thought of hurting Mason, I knew I had to get out of that house. I broke up with him, packed all my stuff, and moved out that day. The truth was, I knew I was going to respond to Adam's message. I didn't feel I had the strength not to, and I didn't want Mason to get dragged into whatever mess that would create. I remember being so scared of Adam knowing I lived with Mason, which makes no sense logically because he was married to someone else. I felt guilt for hurting Mason, but I knew I had to go. I was weak and the only thing that got me to move out was knowing Adam was back in any capacity, and I refused to talk to him while being with someone else. Mason was good to me, and I didn't want to be a cheater. I never really talked to him again. I am not the "good guy" in everyone's story. Of course, there is a baffling plot twist, so for your entertainment; years later, Mason got with the same girl Adam married, and they also had a baby together; My life is a? Yea, you remember.

Somehow, someway, after the year of detox I had gone through, I so easily allowed my abuser back into my life. Unfortunately, I know that many will be able to relate as I share this confusing part of my story, which even I find hard to understand.

Abusive relationships are like drug addictions I've found. No matter what you do, or how much wise council you receive from those that you love, ultimately only you are the one that must walk away from the drugs once and for all. Apparently, I hadn't had enough.

Adam's baby was tiny. Like, newborn tiny when I saw him again. The fact that I held the baby that he had with some random girl he cheated on me with and married is beyond me, but I did. I felt nothing but love for that little boy either. It wasn't his fault he was born into chaos. He was an extension of this person I was trauma-bonded with, this person I loved. That's the thing about my heart I had to learn.

I wasn't fazed by anything. What I understand now is we can only truly love another to the depths we love ourselves, and I loved myself very little. I loved myself so little I allowed unimaginable treatment because, on some level, I felt I deserved it.

> *Trauma bond-Trauma bonding, in contrast, describes an unhealthy type of attachment toward a person that causes trauma. More specifically, trauma bonding relationships are perpetuated by cycles of abuse, followed by love and kindness.*

Thankfully, this lapse in judgement didn't take me long to figure out this time. I had just started in a network marketing nutrition company I really believed in and was excited about. He made fun of it, and for the first time, the belief I had in my future was enough to slowly pull me away from his grasp. He seemed terrified of his ex and cautioned me to be careful because he didn't want her to hurt me. (If you're wanting to take a time machine and ask me what in the h e double hockey sticks, I was possibly thinking, just hop in, I would like to go with you.)

I took calls from the jail for a few weeks when some drama between Adam and his ex landed him in there. A beautiful, driven, young girl with her entire life in front of her, starting a new business, deciding on college with endless opportunity and choice, taking calls from the jail, from an abusive narcissist with a newborn, and an ex-wife. W-T-F.

The very last straw came on Super Bowl Sunday. I was so excited to go to this football party because finally we had mutual friends. We were going to my new friend Zoe's house. She also was in the network marketing company I had joined and worked at the smoothie shop I had just started working at. Her husband played softball with Adam, and they had been friends for years. We rode to the party in my car. Adam drove because it was far out in the country, and I had no idea how to get us there. We arrived early to help set up. The party was in their basement and a few of the guys were already down there setting up the TVs. I headed upstairs to help Zoe and a few other girls cook and get all the food ready. Two hours went by, and we headed down with the food to find quite a few people had already arrived. My body shuddered when I heard "Hey babe!" and realized Adam was somehow already drunk. He came over and I forced a smile and said, "Whatcha been doing down here?" He slurred something about playing pool and tried to grope all over me. I lightly pushed him off, which he didn't like, and he started picking me up more aggressively, telling me to watch how I talk to him. I could feel eyes on us, so I tried to control the situation like I always did, calmly asking him to put me down until one of the other girl's husbands sternly said "Adam," demanding he relax. His eyes were strong, silently communicating that he wasn't asking. He was one of the ones that knew. One of the ones brave enough to say something and I was grateful, because a lot of people never did. Adam laughed it off, saying "come on man, I'm just playing!" and went to play another game of pool. I was good at putting a face on and concealing feelings at the point, so I turned and started a conversation with a group of girls near me, shoving it all down deep, my inner performer skills shining.

I headed back upstairs with Zoe and helped her with the dishes while the party continued. I would have done anything to get away from Adam when he was like that. When we opened the door to the basement, I heard him yelling about a bonfire party he was going to loudly and annoyingly asking who was joining him.

As we came down the stairs in what felt like slow motion, I saw him stumbling from left to right, holding a case of beer. His eyes met mine and with an evil smile he threw up his middle finger, "FUCK YOU PENELOPE!" He yelled at me across the room, the people sober enough to notice looking at me in shock and him in disgust. I froze because, what else do you do with that? He kept yelling stupid things as he headed for the door with my keys, and I ran across the room towards him. The same friend that stopped him last time, this time, stopped me. "Let him go," he said.

"Not in my car." I replied.

Zoe's husband fought him for the keys and told him to get out. Someone else must have taken him to the party because he was gone in the next few moments. His friend handed me my car keys with sympathy in his eyes, and Zoe looked at me in horror.

"You can stay with me upstairs," she said. It's dark and the roads are so curved you won't easily find your way out. You can go home when it's daylight."

I was so numb at that point I don't even think I cried. I remember staring at the ceiling in the dark lying on her couch unable to sleep and processing that number one: My boyfriend had left me in the middle of nowhere with people I hardly knew to go to a bonfire party he was probably cheating on me at, and number two; this person was my boyfriend, and I was allowing it.

Adam's hand startled me awake as he forcefully shoved me, trying to make space on the couch. "Scoot over, baby," he slurred. He reeked of alcohol and bonfire smoke. "You have got to be kidding me," I thought. Embarrass me to no end, treat me like absolute trash, then have the guts to climb into bed with me hours later. As I type this now, my first thought is exactly that, "Are you kidding?" Then a more sobering truthful thought; Of course, he did. How many times before did he do something horrific only to be let right back in? A note for my younger self, and you, my dear reader; You teach people how to treat you. You show people what you will allow and what you won't.

You are responsible for creating boundaries, or you will get to experience people run all over you however they please.

Finally, I had had enough. I leaned back on the couch and kicked him away from me. The floor shook when he fell on the ground and thankfully; he didn't fight back. At that point, I kind of wished he did because I was ready to give it all I had. Adam was so drunk and tired I don't think he had it in him, and he knew our friends were sleeping feet away. Another reason I had the courage that I did. Sliding to the foot of the couch, he started saying the worst things that's ever been said to me. The most terrible, hateful words you can imagine. He just went on, and on and on. Tears rushing out of my eyes, I grabbed my phone and opened the notes app and started writing down everything he said. I remember thinking, "write it all down and read it any time you think for a second to ever let him near you again."

He eventually stopped and passed out. The fear and pain rushed through my body, and I stared out a window until I eventually fell asleep too. I slept for what felt like minutes, and my eyes flashed open as soon as light came through the blinds. I slowly crawled off the couch, terrified to make a noise because of one thing I was certain: I was leaving without him. "Penelope," Adam said my name and my whole body froze before I made it out the door. "I'm going to the bathroom and gonna grab my bag and then we will go," he said. I wouldn't be surprised if he had a zero memory of the night before. He rarely did. When he went to the bathroom, I darted for Zoe's bedroom. I begged her husband to get me safely to my car without him.

I reached for the door handle when he came barreling out of the house. I could tell he was getting ready to yell at me, but always forced a front when people were around. My friend's husband reached up his hand towards him and said, "let her go, I'll take you home."

"Like hell you're leaving without me!" he yelled. My friend's husband looked back at me and said, "go now." I shut the door hearing him yell and watching him charge for the car, hitting the window while my friend's husband grabbed his shoulders, holding him back.

I kept my head forward and started to pull away, afraid of what would happen and simultaneously so incredibly grateful for someone's help. I almost had a heart attack when I heard a loud crash realizing he was softball pitching full beer cans, trying to bust my back windshield as I drove away. I drove the whole forty-five minutes home in silence and cried.

Freedom

Adam called and texted me a million times every day and I worried about ever living a life free of anxiety. I had started my first semester at the local community college and was miserable. I was going for early childhood education because I had always been called to teaching, and I loved children. However, during the few weeks I attended classes, I realized how strongly I disliked rules and any kind of system. I had been working at Subway since I was sixteen, and wearing a uniform, being told what to do, and clocking in and out was slowly killing my spirit day after day. Halfway through that fall semester, I realized I would never make it. I knew I would be incapable of finishing the next three years of courses, and I knew I would suffocate in a school system. My soul was finally beginning to come through strong enough for me to pay attention. I was like a caged animal, desperately needing to be set free into the wild. That's why network marketing was so appealing to me. It represented freedom. I dreamed of being my own boss and simultaneously was coming to the realization that my survival depended on being passionate about what I was doing. I was designed for entrepreneurship, and, with my limited resources, network marketing gave me a fighting chance, and for that I will be forever grateful.

That was the first (and only) semester of college I made it through. I happily dropped out. My parents, however, were not as thrilled. This was the beginning of me following my intuition. I began to awaken to the soul within my body. This was the beginning of me going against the grain, making decisions others would not understand until later. I was certain I would be successful, even though I had no proof to show for it yet.

I was doing well in my business, and I was so incredibly confident and passionate. Finding a new mission and purpose I, for the first time since my sports career ended, was clear where I was going. I wanted my own smoothie location and had a vision of building a massive organization. There was a strong desire to get out of my hometown, and I needed to get away from Adam. No matter how much I knew, or what he did, he was still an addiction; one that I had been fighting since I was fifteen. Leaving town and starting my own life was the best plan in my eyes, but I didn't have a lot of money and very few connections. I was making about two thousand dollars a month, but that would be cut in half if I left the physical location I worked at. An opportunity arose to do a nine-week phlebotomy program. I figured it would give me some sort of skill if I needed to work part-time while building my business, and there were hospitals everywhere. The schooling was only a few hours a day, and I could get the class done quickly. The only issue was, I hated blood lol. I was nauseous every single day of that program. We had to practice on each other for weeks. It's making me want to pass out just thinking about it. I never used the certification or looked for a job. However, I figured there was some reason I was led to learn those skills and I would use it someday.

One connection of somewhere far enough away, but close enough to drive to, was my best option. Jackson's parents lived in West Virginia and were kind enough to offer me a small bedroom and time to stay with them for a while so I could work towards my dream without having to figure out rent and cost of living as soon as I got there.

Everyone knew about my exciting new venture, except few knew the darkness I was running from. I said my goodbyes, hugged my parents, kissed my dog and cat, and packed up my car, ready for my road trip.

No one would have understood what I did next, so I kept it to myself. However, it was something I needed to do, and I'm very grateful I did it.

I called Adam's Mom. I wanted to know that she and her husband would be home, so I had some safety, and when she agreed, I called and asked to see him. I asked for him to come out to my car and he got in my passenger side.

I kept the car parked and looked into the blue eyes that started the whole thing. I felt like it was a time warp back to those early summer nights. His eyes were soft, and the pain within him was all over his face.

Remember, *hurt people hurt people.*

Confidently, I told him I was leaving town, and he didn't need to know where. I told him this would be the last time he ever saw or talked to me. I told him I forgave him for everything he had ever done, and tears started rolling down his face. I told him I hoped he would have a good life with his son, but I would no longer have any part in it, and possibly to your surprise, I thanked him. I thanked him for our time together and it is all these years later I now understand what a lesson and teacher he was for me in fulfilling my life's purpose. Kissing him lightly as if to seal the end of an era, I told him goodbye. I never saw him again. Driving away, I felt like Super Woman; feeling like I had taken off a fifty lb. weight. A lot of traumas to heal ahead of me, however; I was finally on a fresh path.

Unfortunately, a few years later, I heard he spent years in prison for domestic violence. Wherever he is now, I pray he finds healing and is on to a better life.

Lessons Sexual Trauma

One in six US women and one in thirty-three of US men have experienced attempted/ completed rape as a child or an adult, and so many never tell anyone about it. I shared this part of my story to honor anyone that's ever been violated in any way. I want you to know, no matter how "small" or how horrific, I want you to know you are seen. It was not your *fault,* and you did not deserve it.

Suicide

I have some trauma around this topic, and I would only like to speak about it once, so I will share everything here.

Adam was threatening suicide in an attempt to control and manipulate me.

My nervous system was wrecked constantly, and I carried so much pressure and fear of "being the reason" someone ended their life. This wouldn't be the first time I was in a relationship with someone who had mental health issues. If you reading this, relate to loving someone struggling in this way, know I am giving you the biggest hug. Really take a moment and feel my energetic embrace. I want to see and acknowledge you for the pain you've experienced if you ever thought for a second that was your weight to carry. It's important to understand that if something were to happen in this situation, it would not have been my responsibility. This took me a long time to fully accept. Someone threatening or committing suicide cannot be your *fault*. Mental health issues are very serious and very real. I was in another relationship where my partner didn't threaten me with it at all. He hid it from me. He struggled deeply and silently.

I have walked in my home to find a gun laying on the table, and I've seen a rope tied where attempts were almost completed. I have lived in extreme fear of coming home. I have checked the woods and the closets in fear of finding my partner hanging there. I have felt the pain of seeing a partner be in that kind of darkness not knowing how to help them, and I have felt the torture of taking all the responsibility for it.

I have had to work through many traumas of taking responsibility for another's pain or issues. The priest I had in church my entire life growing up jumped off a building when I was twenty years old, sending me into a deep questioning of all I had ever been taught. I don't know who needs to hear this, but it was their path, and you couldn't stop it. If it was a partner, a friend, a parent, or even a child, you are not responsible. I acknowledge I don't have the right to speak on any scenario I haven't experienced. However, this is consequential for you to hear. You. Cannot. Carry. That. Weight. You live your human experience and make mistakes like everyone else. If you have loved someone who's struggled in this way, I ask you please to free yourself from blame, because it will eat you alive. Your life does not deserve to end because of anyone else's decision. I don't know your story, and your pain is warranted. However, I strongly believe if it is not in your control, you deserve peace. There are some things we cannot make sense of, or ever understand. What we can do is do our best to be kind and do our best to treat everyone with love because we have no idea what goes on behind closed doors. Even if it's the closest person to you, you don't know what they are facing inside.

We can do our best to remember we are all human, and reflections of one another, and we can forgive ourselves when we forget that and fall short.

If you, the one reading this, struggle or have struggled with thoughts of suicide, know I am giving you the biggest hug. Really take a moment and feel my energetic embrace. I want to see and acknowledge you for the pain you are feeling or have felt if you ever thought for a second the world would be better without you, because that is not true. If you ever have had thoughts or felt a pain so deep, you felt you had no way out. I beg you to seek help. There is no need for shame. The world needs you.

Suicide and Crisis Lifeline US 988 Call or Text

Addiction

One of my siblings has battled a drug addiction for many years and for a long time, I held a lot of anger and resentment towards him. I didn't understand the things he would do and felt such judgement and disgust towards his actions. I compared my toxic relationship to that of a drug addiction because, with this relationship; I gained empathy.

I now understood the reasoning behind making decisions that were harmful to me. I understood quitting and relapsing in my own ways. I understood unhealthy attachments and becoming a version of myself I didn't recognize. I share this small paragraph to shed light on the fact we all have addictions and coping mechanisms, and I invite you to open your eyes and realize one is no better than the other. My sibling struggled with drugs, I coped with an unhealthy partnership. Maybe you drink, binge watch tv or social media, watch porn, or eat excessively. I invite you to a lens of compassion with the people in your life, and to realize you aren't better or worse than anyone else. Judgement does nothing for the collective. Love, support, and seeing yourself in another is truly the way to change the way we treat each other, and to overcome all levels and layers of unhealthy addiction.

Judgement is useless; however, boundaries are necessary. I invite you to a compassionate lens, however, I strongly encourage whatever boundaries needed for your safety.

Peace

I went back to see Adam that day because when I drove away, it was in peace. I made a conscious decision to take my power back. Without that meeting, I would have felt as if I was running away.

A constant look over the shoulder, and I was ready to be done with the haunting. I am very present to some people are in situations where they do have to run away. There are more severe circumstances where abusers will search for you, but I didn't feel that was the case with him and I. There was an unspoken understanding to let me go. I also knew with all the circumstances he was facing, he had other fish to fry. The way I see human beings is both beautiful and has gotten me into a lot of trouble over the years. I had begun my journey with personal development, and I learned about forgiveness in a book I was reading, and it resonated. Just as I shared in my childhood chapter, I understood holding on to anger or resentment for him in my eyes would have been like drinking poison myself and expecting him to die. Forgiving him was for me. I don't have the capacity for hatred, I never have. I am highly empathetic, and I see humans at their soul level. I've always had an innate understanding that people are not their actions. The skill I was beginning to learn through this relationship was discernment. Discernment in understanding just because I could see light in someone didn't mean I should allow their darkness to my detriment in hopes of saving them. This wouldn't be the end of this lesson.

Jim Rohn said, *"I used to think I'll make them successful even if it kills me."* Then he shockingly says, *"and I almost died! I realized I shouldn't do that anymore."* This was a bad habit the people pleaser in me cultivated with everyone around me. A desire to save them all, unknowingly trying to save myself.

Understand that it's not up to you to save anyone else. Another lesson from Jim Rohn that illustrates a beautiful example is his example of the oxygen masks on a plane. The flight attendant comes over the loudspeaker and says, "in case of emergency, remember to put your mask on first before assisting others." They tell you that because it is innate in many of us to put everyone else's needs before our own.

The reality is if you go trying to save everyone on the plane without any oxygen, you're not going to be able to breathe, which means you'll quickly pass out and not be able to help anyone. What is best for you? What decisions feel good in your body, in your heart? Get used to checking in and asking, "Where am I sacrificing pieces of myself, and why am I doing that?" Unconditional love will not require unhealthy sacrifice.

Earth Angels

In retelling, it is so clear to me the angels that came into my life at the right time, disguised as people. The Coaches that saw a light in me and gave me something to believe in. My childhood best friend that showed up for me and loved me unconditionally all throughout high school, regardless of what mess I was in or how I treated him. Mason and Andrea giving me a family in a dark time. The business owners that offered me a job and an opportunity. My friend Zoe, and her husband protecting me. Adam's mom grabbing my shoulder's telling me to go. My mom always letting me come back, regardless of the disagreements we had. My dad giving me his blessing to go for my dreams; Jackson's family offering me a place to live. So many more examples, but to name a few and bring awareness and gratitude to the angels that were always there.

CHAPTER FOUR

A FRESH START

I saw my small-town fade away in my rearview mirror as I set off on my new adventure. I didn't know where life would take me, however,

I knew I would never be back; visiting my parents would be the extent. I had known since childhood I was not meant to stay there for long.

The following months were some of the most character-building times of my life. I have gone through periods of solitude a few times, and they are always the times I learn the most. This being the first significant.

When I started my network marketing journey, I expected support. If one of my friends or family started a business, I would hype them up and do whatever possible to support them. I found this was not the case for my circle. I got teased, few took me seriously, and even some of my closest friends bought my products off Amazon instead of supporting and ordering from me. When I moved, it was almost as if I had disappeared. Someone from my hometown started a rumor about me "fat-shaming" someone which was not true, and I lost half of my clientele, lowering my income significantly. I felt betrayed and alone. I understand after experiencing these times of solitude, they are divinely orchestrated. God cleaning house. I had a fire, a passion, and a new vision for wanting to do something great, and the people I was surrounding myself with were not on the same path. When you start growing and changing, losing people is often the tradeoff. If you do the things necessary to keep people that are no longer meant for you, you lower your energy to a frequency you've outgrown, and hold yourself back from your destiny. I didn't want to go to the bars, I didn't watch Netflix, I didn't eat fast-food anymore, and I didn't look around my small town and see anyone's life that I desired. I spent my time working out, reading books, and setting goals; I wanted to build a business. There is no ego about it, and I'm not shaming anyone's lifestyle. I don't feel there is any right or wrong way to live your life. If my circle was happy with their day-to-day, great! Everyone gets to live whatever life they desire. However, I knew I had outgrown my environment. I was trying to fit in with people and things I didn't resonate with, so I removed myself. Growth is lonely and painful at times, and I share for someone reading who may not understand this part yet and may find themselves like I did during this time; confused.

When you begin separating yourself and growing, a natural response for the people closest to you is panic. They have the same instinctual response I did in the second grade to keep the tribe together and to keep you where it is comfortable for them. There is an analogy I love sharing about crabs in a bucket. If you place a bunch of crabs in a bucket, they will begin climbing on one another to get out. If one comes close to escape, the rest of the crabs will band together to capture it and pull it back down with the rest. People are the same. Sometimes this is out of fear of you getting hurt, sometimes this is fear they have of losing you. Sometimes it's out of jealousy and insecurities they have of not being as brave, or motivated, or disciplined as you are. Regardless of the reason, you cannot allow yourself to be pulled back into the bucket. I share this so you understand what I wish I would have sooner. There is nothing wrong with growing and changing. You aren't being punished even if it is disguised as that. You are blessed.

God, Spirit, your angels, whatever you believe in, are playing defense. They are removing chains so you can move forward, and you must understand that in the process of the clean-up, you will be alone for a short time. This is where we build character.

Solitude

I unpacked my stuff in the back bedroom of my stepdad's parents' house and asked myself, "okay now what?" I remember sobbing out of the overwhelm of the silence. I did it. I left, I moved, I had arrived, and now had no clue where to begin.

I started with something that didn't seem so daunting, getting a gym membership. If I was going to build a network, I had to go somewhere to meet people. I got a membership at the YMCA and started lifting and going to yoga. I spent a lot of time working out because I was very unclear of what else I should do. Knowing how to run my business back at home was easy for me because I had a structure. I conducted fit camps, organized weight loss challenges, and invited people for smoothies and teas. I was a big fish in an itty bitty pond at home, and now I was a minnow in a great big Southern Ocean.

Thankfully, Jackson's family were very supportive and volunteered to be my first clients. His mom and sister both bought a program, lost weight, and would tell their co-workers about me, and I really appreciated the encouragement.

Ignorance on fire. I am so grateful for how naïve I was because if I understood how daunting the task I was after, it may have prevented me from trying. The only direction I really had was a training event our company held one time a month, and a couple of my up lines I could call for questions. Through the events, books, trial and error, and Google, I failed my way through learning everything about nutrition, fitness, and business. Selling nutrition products, I figured the better physical results I had, the better I could attract people who wanted me to coach them. I developed an obsession, exercising for extended periods and having a limited food intake. I would consume the products, and eat meal preps of tilapia and broccoli, occasionally some rice. Insufficient eating led me to develop an unhealthy obsession with my weight and body image.

Full of positive tenacious energy, I began attempting to grow my business. I typed up business cards and would get dressed up, going into businesses offering free in-services. In-services were a way I was taught to network and gain clientele from the trainings I attended. I would offer to set up a day and time, bring in samples of the shakes and teas, explaining the benefit of the product and what I would offer as a coach. I would tell them about the smoothie location I had in Ohio and paint them my vision to duplicate the same thing. I would then confidently share my plans of opening multiple locations and changing the health habits of the community.

No one was interested. My discouragement grew with each no, and my confidence was quickly fading. This was also the first time since I was fifteen that I didn't have a boyfriend, and hardly anyone to talk to. The defeat, loneliness, and anxiety from the massive life change began to set in, as well as the stress I was putting on myself with my body image.

I started a vicious cycle of binge-eating that did as much, if not more, damage to me mentally than physically. I started starving myself for days at a time until I would cave and eat everything in sight.

I started gaining weight in the forms of body fat and shame. Coping mechanisms come in all forms and I've read many perfectionists and over achievers fall victim to eating disorders.

I was beginning to spiral, and I wasn't making any money. I think my family could see me starting to crack, so my aunt offered to get me a hosting job. "You would work evenings, so you could build your business during the day, and make some money in the afternoons. It could also help you meet people!" she said, assuring me.

I was willing to try anything because I felt like I was going insane. I started as a hostess in a fancy restaurant at the local casino. They had to give me a special badge because I was nineteen years old, not even old enough to *be* in a casino. I had to dress up, and wear heels every night. My work schedule started at around 4:30 pm and I usually got home around 11:00. Standing there all night was a terrible experience. I hated the whole thing. With a forced smile, I would welcome guests, then walk them to their table and the three feet back. Despite hating the job, I met some enjoyable people in the kitchen and was happy to have a few new friends to interact with.

This went on for a few weeks and I was picking up bad habits like sleeping in, eating unhealthy food, and scrolling social media for hours. I was losing my ambitious stamina and feeling guilt and pressure to succeed, once again living from a place of proving my worth to the world.

I was at my little cousin's basketball game when someone placed an order from my website. The profit was equal to the check I had just received from the restaurant, and I had an epiphany. To earn the check from the restaurant, I put makeup on, drove 35 minutes in traffic, stood in heels all night, got yelled at by a grouchy boss, drove another 35-40 minutes home and did that for two weeks; an average, including a drive time of 7.5 hours a day. To earn the same amount in retail profit, I answered some messages while relaxing at my cousin's basketball game, taking about twenty minutes. A lightbulb went off for me and I never again worked a regular job. My inspiration relit, despite my painfully low confidence.

Lessons

The main thing that kept me going was my commitment to personal development. I read books or listened to motivational videos all day long. I would read story after story about successful people failing countless times before making it, holding on to the faith that if I kept going, things would get better. I embraced the mindset of allowing myself time to learn. If I would have gone to school, I would have spent four-seven years reading books and taking tests before anyone expected me to be making money. It made perfect sense to me that my success in this may not be any different. While attending one of our trainings, I heard someone from stage talking about giving it five years no matter what, so I was in. (Ironically, that person I believe if I remember correctly was Elijah, an invisible string to each other all along) I cried constantly, and faced countless rejections, but I was in.

The skills and strength I gained from these experiences are far more than I could have gotten from a book. This season is where I got comfortable with rejection. This season made me resilient. This season is where I developed people skills. With every conversation, I learned how to talk. I learned how to look people in their eyes and read body language. I went from walking in with my shoulders down, terrified, voice shaking, to being able to stand tall and articulate with words. I learned how to move forward. I lost my friends, I didn't have a boyfriend, I lost clients, I heard "no" every single day. I felt stupid, I felt like a failure, I felt no one took me seriously because of my age. I felt completely lost. I doubted myself every day, *and* I kept going. I realize now it built an incredible character inside of me. I was training for life, and I was learning. I was a bamboo tree; I just didn't know it yet. Bamboo trees take five years to grow, and they must be watered and fertilized every day. The interesting thing about them is they don't show any progress or break through the ground at all until the five-year mark. After the five years of consistent water and fertilization, the tree grows ninety feet tall in a matter of five weeks! The tree grows the whole time, you just can't see it. All the reading, trying, failing, crying, and practicing was my version of water and fertilizer. I was discouraged because I couldn't yet see any sign of a tree but continued holding the faith that the time for my bamboo to rise would come.

This is a perspective I have carried into every season of my life. I trust my hard work, consistency, and patience. I trust the promise of a harvest in any area I'm working in, even when there is no sign of a tree. It has proven true time and time again, and any successful person will tell you the same. Many people give up too quickly. Many people fail to do the work. Many people fall short of the discipline of watering every day and wonder why they never see a tree. My lesson here is one of hard work and belief always paying off. The growth is happening beneath the surface if you are consistent. You must believe in what you are doing so strongly no one can tell you any different if you want to make it. You must show up day in and day out with your vision clear about where you're going. I knew I wanted to do something big. I knew I wanted to be a successful entrepreneur and impact people and I believed in my core it would happen, and there was zero proof. I was awkward, insecure, broke, had no clue what I was doing or saying, but I was going for it. Unknowingly, I was training. I was developing skills, rejection, knowledge, and experience. I was reading books every single day that were developing and changing my thoughts.

Every night I got ready and did my hair and makeup; I was getting better at it. Every night, I worked as a hostess. I learned how to be comfortable talking to people and got better at making people laugh as they sat down. Every time I faced rejection when offering a business in-service and had the strength to go into the next one, my skin got tougher. As I went to the gym, I was building muscle slowly and surely. With each book and podcast I listened to, I was getting smarter and strengthening my belief in myself. Each skill I developed in this time I would use later when new opportunities arose. If I hadn't gone through each of these experiences and had the training, I wouldn't be ready when the time came to capitalize on my dreams. We never know when that time may come. How long I would need to work until my dreams came to fruition didn't matter. It was the belief of where I was going that was guiding me and helped me to drown out the noise of any inner or outer critics. Instilling lasting change and working towards a dream or a goal is a daily effort. A *journey*. Watering that tree and growing beneath the surface for as long as it takes, surrendering to when or how your tree will come.

CHAPTER FIVE

MY HERO

Just as my ambition battery was fading, it was time for another one of our success training seminars and I couldn't wait to be there. They gave me hope and inspiration and helped me not feel so alone in my big dreams. I would road trip the three and a half hours and show up bright and bushy tailed with my notebook ready to learn.

So, there was a guy. Let's call him Dean.

Are you surprised? Of course not. I was a little lover, full of codependence, trying to fulfill the prophecies in my belief backpack. If I was going to meet my prince and fall in love anywhere, this would be the place to do it. Someone driven like me, someone into health and fitness. It made perfect sense. I harbored a crush on him for about a year, jokingly predicting to my friends he would be my boyfriend. I would show them his Facebook profile photo because it happened to be a shirtless picture of him sporting what I swear must have been fourteen abs. Never had I seen someone with a twelve pack of abs in my life.

We hadn't talked much because the one time we did, I found out how old he was, and I decided I had finally met someone I felt was *too* old for me. He would always smile at me or stare at me, but we kept our distance, only seeing each other on event days. He was fourteen years older than me, which was shocking because he didn't look it at all, and our personalities clicked so naturally.

This was the event I decided I no longer cared about the age difference because I wanted to talk to him, so I did. He invited me, his brother, and his brother's girlfriend to a casual dinner after the event and we started texting back and forth following that weekend. Talking to him gave me a breath of fresh air because I finally had met someone who was on the same page. He had just moved from his hometown to a town over about an hour away, where he also didn't know anyone. He moved to be closer to his son. I had decided during childhood I didn't want to be with anyone that had other kids or a blended family because of my experience. However, I already liked him, and I realized how fast ideals of what you think your life should look like can change. No longer caring about the age difference, I admired that he was a good dad. I cared about the person he was above all else.

He was so kind; a recurring trait that you have more than likely gathered by now I note first in anyone I've ever been attracted to. His passion for dreaming aligned with my purpose. Our goals aligned perfectly. He was funny, and our personalities complimented each other. Dean was in a similar position to me; new place, trying to build a business, and alone. We were passionate about fitness and personal growth, and I fell for him quickly. I had just come out of a four- year nightmare with Adam, and a confusing period of random attempted "dating" and loneliness. I was trying to make my dreams come true while in a place I didn't feel I belonged in the least. My life felt so cold, and he felt like warmth. Although unconventional, he was exactly what I wanted in a partner, and I remember feeling like God sent him to save me.

Dean and I dated long distance for only two months when he asked me to move there. I had met his son a few times and loved him. He had Type One Diabetes and had to take insulin shots. The phlebotomy course I never used, and the ability to stab a needle into someone's skin, finally came in handy when I would need to help him.

My anxiety about a baby momma was soon calmed when I met her, and thank God, we got along great.

He lived about six hours from where I was living in West Virginia. Is moving in with someone you've been dating for a few short months the smartest idea? Probably not. However, being together felt a lot better than braving this dream on our own, and if you haven't figured it out yet, I had a tendency of leaping first and figuring it out later.

I packed up my car, thanked my family profusely for their hospitality, and called my dad on the drive. "Hey dad, I need you to sit down. I have something to talk to you about."

I wanted him seated for fear he may have a stroke for what I was about to say and didn't want him knocking himself out from the fall lol. "So, dad." I began. "I'm just going to lay it on you full stop, no brakes. I have a boyfriend. He's quite a bit older than me, and he has a kid. I am moving back to Ohio to be with him, and I'm sure you're probably worried but you don't need to be because I know his family, he works for the company I work for, he's a good person, we are going to build a big business together."

There was a long pause, and I braced myself for his response.

"How old is the kid? And how old is he!?" he asked, concerned for my sanity.

When I reflect on all these parts of my life, I can absolutely see everyone's constant concern for me. However, I always know what I'm doing. If for some reason I'm off, I course correct and learn from the experience for my benefit relatively quickly. When everyone around me is freaking out, I'm usually calm because I am in tune with my inner knowing. I was meant for a bit of chaos. My soul relishes in it. Trusting my inner voice got easier when it became louder than the outside world.

My dad was mainly concerned about Dean's son because of the stress he understood about being a stepparent. My mom was worried I was going to be murdered. Regardless, they knew I was going to do what I was going to do. My parents had come to terms with which they were never going to control my crazy self and I think secretly they may enjoy the element of surprise I bring to their lives.

I moved in and we got to work on our big dreams. I convinced Dean to quit his job and go all in on our network marketing vision probably much sooner than we should have, but hey, no risk, no reward, right?

"Fortune favors the bold,"- Terence

Humble Beginnings

We were broke for months, but we were happy. We tried everything to build our business, we even started a fit camp at the local park in March. If you've never experienced March in Ohio, there is usually snow on the ground. Dean and I went into every business and distributed flyers. We tried social media, and did more in-services, all with little to no traction. Sticky notes with the layout of our dream business production, pictures of our marketing plan levels, and a giant vision board of everything we were going to achieve plastered the walls of our one- bedroom apartment. Our resources were limited, but our belief was strong.

One story to emphasize the belief we had was our couch story. When I moved in, Dean had porch furniture in the living room, and the couch I specifically hated. It was two pieces of plywood with a cushion on it.

We went to a weekend training where the guest speaker shared a section on loving your environment. He talked about how our environment affected our mindset, and if there were things in our house giving us bad vibes, we should get rid of them and trust the universe would bless us with things we *did* want. He was probably referring to throw pillows or clutter you may have lying around, but we have to remember; I am dramatic.

I was sold. Go hard or go home. This was the perfect opportunity for me to burn that couch, haha! We cleared out all our furniture. All of it. We took it all to the dump high from the adrenaline of manifesting our dream life! We were taking videos and laughing, blaring music on the drive back, envisioning our successful future!

It was all fun and games until we were still eating our dinner crisscross applesauce in our empty living room with Dean glaring at me, really wanting a chair to sit on three weeks later. Most impulsive decisions fueled by yours truly. I digress. I share to show the level of commitment we were in mentally.

I remember the first birthday I had when we lived together. My birthday is on the twelfth and we got paid from our company on the fifteenth. After paying bills, we were usually struggling by the first of the next month. I remember Dean coming home with a single cupcake he got from the grocery store and splitting it for me and his son, I remember making a wish blowing out those candles envisioning all that I knew the future would be, and the faith I had that the current reality would be temporary. I wished what I already knew inside to be true, that we would make it.

Our efforts weren't working, and I believed we needed our own smoothie location to make anything happen. He had built one from the ground up in his hometown, and I thrived when I was in mine, and had missed it so much ever since leaving. The issue with a brick-and-mortar location is you need some sort of money to open it. Dean was all for my idea, but more of a realist in the sense of we really didn't have any money. We discovered that we would receive a few thousand dollars from a tax refund, and I managed to secure a $5,000 loan with my dad as a co-signer.

My dad believed in me even though he didn't understand, and for that I will be forever thankful.

Dean and I had been together for about seven months when he asked me to marry him. There wasn't a big proposal or any ring. We were sitting on the couch laughing and he asked with a smile, "do you want to get married?" I didn't think twice about it. Our relationship was so natural, and I had wanted to get married my whole life. I loved him, and he and his son were my family now, so I said yes. I wore a cheap little gemstone ring for the time being and was happy. There was one nagging thought in the back of my mind, however. One that I buried in fear of it ruining my fairytale. "I wasn't first."

There it was. Coming back to haunt me. My new fiancé worshipped the ground I walked on. However, whenever an argument or something came up, that would put me and his son at odds, from my perspective, his son came first, and would always come first. Regardless of this mentality being irrational or not, it was a knowing within me that something wasn't right, and I buried it. Intuition can only be ignored for so long.

We found an affordable place to rent for our new business that had previously been a dog grooming studio. It was a mess, and we had our work cut out for us, so we got started. We did everything ourselves. Multiple 24-hour straight nights painting the walls until one of us would see stars and go home to sleep and stay with his son while the other took a shift. Dean did all the electrical and almost killed us both on more than one occasion lol. We were gifted tables and chairs we spray painted and got the cheapest blenders we could find. The day the plumbing inspection passed, and we had water, I bawled my eyes out. That place was our dream, and I was so incredibly proud of it for all the blood, sweat, and tears we put into it. I posted a photo of the first shake we made there at about 10:00PM one night and said something along the lines of, "first shake of millions."

And I was right.

We opened our first location in August and our business exploded. We started creating such an impact in our community growing by the day. All the flyers and invitations we had done the months prior got our name out enough that when the "crazy fitness people" who were working out in the park had a physical location, the people came.

We had such a charming, dynamic together. We were a young, attractive, fit couple full of positivity, life, love, and kindness with a mission to change lives. People fell in love with us.

We eloped in September, and by eloped, I mean we decided a few days prior, and got married in our officiant's backyard. I was twenty years old. We bought a fake diamond from JC Penny's, and I got my dress the day before the wedding at TJ Maxx. I spent more on a bow tie for my stepson than I did on my dress, and we ate chicken wings after. It was perfect. The only people at our wedding were Dean's sister, her husband, their dad, and my new stepson. I felt a twinge of pain that day not having my family there, however we talked about having a "real" wedding later when we could afford to. Yet again I buried the off feeling. I got pregnant with our son in December of the same year. I had excessive sickness the entire nine months and went from high achieving boss fitness Barbie to spending my days trying to keep any food down. I experienced a few hospital visits and a terrifying experience with some nausea medicine. Google "dystonia" if you need a good laugh, it led to one wild and later hilarious experience.

Thankfully, by that time we had already gained an incredible team of people and employees that turned into a family for us, helping keep the business afloat.

Miracle

I had the easiest birth I could imagine, and the day my son was born will forever be the best day of my life. Creedence (Creed) Michael came into the world and changed my heart forever.

He is the greatest blessing I have ever known. I was twenty-one years old.

Michael came from my husband's late mother, *Micha*. There was this divine moment in the hospital where it was so clear his mom was there with us. When you have a baby, they have these little security tags with the baby's social, birthdate, and a random sequence of numbers for security of the baby so they don't get switched or somehow taken. Creed's random code was my husband's mom's birthdate.

I remember him staring at it in disbelief when he told me, and you could feel the presence of something, or someone rather, otherworldly.

The first seven months of Creed's life were some of the happiest moments I have had, and the worst. I had severe postpartum anxiety; To be brief, postpartum is a highly under-communicated topic in our culture and it's very real. The thing about it is it will affect every mom differently, and even every pregnancy differently. Some moms don't seem to be affected. Other moms have severe depression or anger. There are mothers who don't bond with their baby or feel overwhelmed grieving their life before motherhood. In my case, I had extreme anxiety and irrational fear something would happen to him. For example, I feared he would stop breathing or someone would drop him or hurt him. I wasn't cognizant anything was "wrong" because the only knowledge of postpartum I had was horrific stories about moms not wanting their baby anymore. I was the total opposite; I was *obsessed* with my baby. I didn't trust anyone with him, and lost interest in anything that wasn't him. My work was unenjoyable, and I felt anger towards my spouse and stepson for no reason. I also didn't leave my house (or sleep much) due to my mother-bear-like instincts. The anger created separation. I was cold to my husband, and way too harsh with my stepson when I hadn't ever been that way before. Finally, Dean asked me to read about postpartum. I did a Google search, and after realizing I had most of the symptoms on the list, I snapped out of the confusing fog I had been operating in the five months prior.

Over the course of three years, my husband lost both of his parents. He and I were the ones to find his dad after he had a heart-attack and the sound of Dean crying echoing through that apartment when he realized he was gone still shakes me.

Amid the grieving and navigating being parents, we were also business partners.

Our one location turned into seventeen and we were putting every ounce of our energy and effort into the dream. I now found myself leading a large organization of people, with my husband twenty-four hours a day, with two kids, at twenty-three years old.

Building a six-figure business starting from zero that involves pouring belief into others and helping them change their lives is a big feat. We worked our asses off and faced tons of adversity to build what we did, and really helped a lot of people in the process. Being an entrepreneur is not for the weak, and neither is working with your spouse.

I was obsessed with the pursuit of success. Subscribing to a never satisfied mentality that fueled and satiated all the negative beliefs in my belief backpack, I never took a break. I operated solely from my masculine energy most of the time. After I had Creed, there was a drastic change in the dynamic of my relationship with Dean and we quit having much of a romantic connection at all. He was my best friend in the whole world, my business partner, and the best dad. All things I used to hide the harsh reality that we were no longer lovers. Those feelings were too painful for me to come to terms with, so I turned up the over achiever within me and focused on the things that did work for as long as I could. The pressure of it all mounted four years into our marriage and I began to unravel at the seams.

Staring at the ceiling most nights feeling waves of depression and guilt that I would hide, I felt so guilty that my feelings had changed. I had so much anxiety about all the possible outcomes. Staying in a marriage I didn't feel was right gave me anxiety. Hurting the person I loved so deeply and breaking up our family also gave me debilitating anxiety. I was silently consumed for months with this painful knowing of the truth and paralyzed with the ability to act on it.

This was one of the first times I understood that life is not always black and white. I loved my husband, and I had outgrown the version of myself that fit in our marriage. We had gone to therapy; we had read the relationship books; it was not a decision I was coming to lightly. I knew in my soul it was time to move on, and I fought it. I feared the unknown, and I took our commitments seriously. I also have always been a bird. A bird that now felt caged as I stared at the ceiling, unable to sleep night after night thinking about the fact that I was twenty-four years old and made a lifetime commitment that was no longer true for me. I was terrified of the hell I was about to walk through. The hell of hurting him, our kids, and everyone else that looked up to us in this "mom and dad" role we played in our community. I also had a deep understanding by this point in my life: Regardless of the circumstances, when faced with a battle of my desire to please and my freedom, my freedom would always eventually win.

We had been married for four years, but I think we spent more time together than couples who have been married for twenty-five. My side of the story with my marriage and divorce was one of outgrowing a version of myself. I highly underestimated how I would change from age 20 to 25 or how much I've changed from 25 to 30. I attracted a savior at age 20 and by this time I was coming into my independence. The dynamic we had co-created worked for 20-year-old me and started to make 24-year-old me feel small, and I am anything but that. The truth is, he didn't do anything *wrong*; he was relatively the same as he had always been. I changed. Now it was like forcing a puzzle piece into a place it isn't meant to fit in. I viewed the world differently. I wanted different things. *I* was completely different.

A few days before Thanksgiving, I asked for a divorce. It was one of the hardest things I have ever done. I was so broken, and it was so painful to know the pain I was causing, I went completely numb, unwilling to face it.

CHAPTER SIX

POT MEET KETTLE

This is an important chapter sharing some of my tea, so to speak. Shadows. Skeletons in the closet; we all have them, don't we? Maybe a chapter of your life you choose to lock up or not look at. A past version of you that did something you're not proud of, or something that you have a hard time comprehending you were even capable of. I think it's only fair I share mine if I'm going to be so completely open about everything else. My close friends and I call this one "the dark ages." A mid-life crisis at twenty-four- years- old for yours truly. One that I am at total peace with, and non-judgement of as I share it now because the punishment and shame I once put on myself was far worse than anyone else could attempt to.

Loving yourself means loving all parts. The Yin and the Yang. What you or the world at large has deemed "good girl, or good boy" behavior and accepting your darkness. Grace. Giving yourself space to develop and accepting every aspect of you. Looking back and thinking, "What in the hell was I thinking?" and saying "You know what? We live and we learn. When you know better, you do better, and take the lessons that come with it.

Pot meets kettle is the name of this chapter because the girl that was once destroyed by being cheated on became a cheater. Gasp!

I cheated on my husband while we were married, with someone else who was also married.

I met this new person about a month after I asked for a divorce, and he was also going through a divorce. (Which I later found out was a lie)

It's worth mentioning that my husband wasn't faultless, either. Both partners play a role in starting or ending a relationship. He has his own skeletons. I only mention this for the sake of the complete picture. Painting a picture of me with devil horns, and my ex floating around with a halo attached to his head wouldn't be an accurate depiction, however I am not here to air any dirty laundry (that is not pertinent to my story) of someone I desire to peacefully co-parent with.

Regardless of the justifications I made in my head, I was still married and so was this other person. It was an out of character thing that happened and priding myself on loyalty and honesty my whole life I really struggled with confusion on, "how did I get here?"

Have you ever asked yourself that?

"How did I get here?"

It's one of those things they program us to judge. I was ready to vote any cheater I knew straight off the island until I became one. I was convinced I fell for this person; however, it is crystal clear to me now that I was clawing for any distraction to save myself from the immense pain and guilt I was feeling for getting divorced, and finally crumbling under the extreme nonstop pressure, stress, and life changes of the five years prior. Suddenly I understood complexities I hadn't before, and started to really come into clarity that, like I stated earlier, the world truly isn't always black and white. It's possible to develop feelings for someone you're not "supposed to." It's possible to have feelings for multiple people simultaneously. Excitement can temporarily conceal immense grief and sadness. You can be convinced you feel something for someone, only to find out it never had anything to do with them, and you were only looking to escape; or looking to cope with stress and intense pressure you didn't know what to do with. This was the case for me.

This is controversial, however let's talk about Tiger Woods, for example, and no I am not comparing myself to Tiger lol, just offering a perspective. Many people look at him and see a monster. A raging narcissist that hurt a lot of people and ruined his life. I, however, see something different. I see a human. A human that lived his whole life with a rigid controlling father and intense stress and pressures that finally mounted, and he snapped. If you haven't seen his documentary, I highly recommend it. My main point is there is always a lot more to a story, and a lot of information when you go digging into *"How did I get here?"*

I digress.

To be honest, I can't tell you what I was thinking. I don't recall much of this time. A friend invited me to a new gym, and next thing I knew, I was involved in this thrilling, risky affair playing with fire. Not only the chance of hurting other people, but I was knowingly risking my entire business reputation I had just spent years building.

What I had the hardest time coming into forgiveness for myself about was that I felt I needed to lie, and the way I knew I hurt my ex when that was the last thing I wanted to do.

There was guilt, sadness, and an adrenaline rush with the darkness I was dancing with that no matter how much I didn't want to face, was very human. This is where the shadow aspect comes in. Coming to terms with dark thoughts you have, the ability to lie, or whatever else that's a part of you that you or society deems "undesirable." We all have things.

What I'm bringing to light is the shadow aspect of accepting that we are not "good or bad" people. We are humans. Humans do amazing and stupid things. Learning from our mistakes, and facing consequences are a huge part of evolution, however in my opinion, it's the shame that kills us. Shame is poison to the soul, and if we ever desire freedom, we must release it. It's in the same energetic field with hate and resentment. We gotta let that shit go.

To wrap up this story, it all came to light in one big explosion; listen, it always does, and it always will. The truth always comes out in one way or another, and karma is very real. I found out this person I was seeing was also seeing half the gym while "working on things with his wife."

This mounted in a lot of painful conversation with my ex, and out of the desperate, panicked desire to make everything okay again, and fix what I felt I broke-when my ex asked me to give our marriage one more try, I agreed. I silenced my voice once again, and shoved my inner knowing as far down as I possibly could, burying the past with it.

"WHEN YOU KNOW BETTER YOU DO BETTER"
– Maya Angelou

Your past does not define you. Remember that. You aren't any one thing. Your value is not defined by your greatest achievement or worst mistake. You can change, grow, learn, and evolve, and when you know better, DO better- and what is "better" anyway? If you're reading this book, I know you aren't an evil, manipulative monster. I also know you've done things you're not proud of, and you probably have beaten yourself up repeatedly, whether consciously or subconsciously. What I invite you to consider is the shame you're carrying will make you sick if you do not choose to release it. Have you lied to someone? Did you steal a ChapStick from the store when you were nine? Did you bully someone severely in school and do you still carry the weight? Did you really hurt someone and regret it? Did you manipulate a person or situation for your own selfish gain? Did you cheat? Did you do something much "worse" that no one knows about?

Your shadows live inside of you. Once you come into acceptance with all that you are, light and dark, and forgive the past versions of you, you can move forward. This requires truth. This requires pulling back the curtain. The truth sets us free. It may sound cliché, but it's true. The person/people on the other side of your actions may never forgive you, and you cannot control that. Freedom doesn't come without consequence. Forgiveness on their side does not concern you, it is their work. Every experience, "good" or "bad," is growing and developing our soul on its journey. The real lesson is realizing nothing is good or bad, it just is. Those labels will keep you chained if you aren't careful.

For example, if you are married and your partner cheats on you, you have many choices on how to move forward. The beautiful thing about being human is we have free will. Every situation, scenario, and every relationship is different. Life is complex, remember?

How I see it, you have two healthy choices. One is to know you are incapable of trusting them anymore. Being honest about your values at the core and coming to terms with the fact you won't be able to reach a level of intimacy with them again, and although painful, decide to end the relationship. By doing this, you are setting both of you free. Option number two is to forgive them, and I mean really forgive them, and only you will know if this is something you are capable of or not. To love them genuinely, forgive them free of resentment, and move forward into a new version of your relationship; having clear, honest communication about what comes up and what comes next. By doing this, you are also setting both of you free.

Lessons

I learned this lesson first with my toxic relationship with Adam, then again with my marriage. In Adam's example, he would cheat on me, and I would stay with him. My mouth would voice forgiveness; however, my actions would punish. Bringing up the past constantly using it to punish him repeatedly for hurting me. I wasn't taking him back with compassion and unconditional love; I was staying with him out of fear and co-dependence. Of course, I didn't have awareness of this. I was reacting from the pain.

Life I've found is lived forward and understood backwards.

He was the cheater, however at some point I became the abuser in my own way. He caused the pain, but it was on me to either forgive him, or to walk away.

In my marriage, *pot meet kettle*, I was the cheater, and in this scenario my ex voiced he truly forgave me, and I feel he meant it. He didn't punish me going forward; however, I continued punishing myself.

I share that story because whatever you have done; you pay your price, your consequence, then you deserve to be set free. You don't deserve to relive the shame and be kicked repeatedly by yourself, or by anyone else. In my scenario with Adam, the consequence he deserved was losing my love, losing an incredible partner. What he didn't deserve was to be berated about it repeatedly for the following year, regardless of what he had done. In a similar way, once I had come into awareness and snapped out of my reckless behavior and faced it, I didn't deserve the levels of shame and self-hatred I carried long after. I am a human; so are you. We make mistakes. Face your truths, your shadows, and start the path of forgiveness with whom you can control; yourself.

Lyrics from Trevor Hall's *You Can't Rush Your Healing* are coming to me:

> Well, everybody's got that chapter
> Of dark and darker days, yeah
> Saturn seems to be returning
> And his essence can't be tamed
> Some may like to fight it
> Try to plan a secret attack
> But the more you push it
> The more it's pushin' you back
> So, you can't rush your healing
> Darkness has its teachings
> Love is never leaving

CHAPTER SEVEN

DEATH & REBIRTH

We stayed together for one more year and, like I shared, at the time I couldn't forgive myself for the disruption I caused. I also couldn't forgive myself for silencing a truth I knew inside, and for keeping up a facade to keep everyone else happy. The pain inside was overwhelming, so I turned to my familiar way of coping, achievement.

That final year we were together, we achieved many of the dreams we had set out after in the beginning of our relationship. Dean and I reached the top 1% of the company, and another prestigious level called the *one million lifetime achievement award*, which represented a lot of people we personally helped change their health. We achieved a monthly income of $30,000! Our highest earning month on record. Dean bought me my dream Louis Vuitton purse that had been on my vision board for years. We built a brand-new location and designed it piece by piece the way we had always talked about, with a room perfect for my dream office. Champagne bottles popped as we cried tears from years of sacrifice. Our conversations revolved around the decision to buy or build a house, as well as our desired travel destinations. We relished in a comeback tale of a power couple that had fallen from grace, picked up the pieces and had come back stronger than ever. However, beneath the glimmering surface, there was an empty truth.

"I think we should get a divorce," Dean said one afternoon, standing across from me in the kitchen. I looked at him, shocked. "You aren't happy, and I can't live like this," he said.

I had retreated so far into myself; I think part of me had come to terms with burying the bird inside. When I agreed to get back together, I made a silent promise to myself I wouldn't ever put everyone through that kind of pain again, even if that meant sacrificing myself. Of course, this was a very unhealthy belief system. However, it is where I was mentally.

He set me free with his words, and I know it caused him a lot of pain to do it.

What I have come to understand, is he also set himself free. He deserved someone who would touch his back when he was cooking in the kitchen.

He deserved someone who wanted more babies and would stare into his eyes. He deserved the right partner for him, and so did I. What I understand now is although I felt I was honoring him by staying married, really, I was doing the opposite. By staying married to Dean, I was keeping both of us from the life we were meant for, and there's nothing noble about that.

Besides the obvious sadness that comes with divorce, ours had another layer. The story, the dream. We made it. We actually made it to the top of the mountain. We did the thing we spent years manifesting and working towards, and when we finally reached the top, our relationship was over. It felt like a sick joke. The truth was our relationship was only being held together by the relentless pursuit of the dream, and once finally reached, the stitches holding us together burst at the seams. I had some resentment at first towards our dream and even blamed it. "What was the point?" I questioned often. I realized that was a very poor question. Tony Robbins always says, "If you want a better answer, ask a better question." Just because something ends doesn't mean it wasn't worth experiencing.

I grew exponentially during the time I was married. Personally, as a businessperson and a leader. I became a mother, I watched my stepson grow, my ex and I changed many people's lives for the better. We traveled to places like Hawaii and Colorado, went to fancy company parties, spoke on a stage together in front of 30,000 people, and were the catalyst to many communities having a healthy, safe haven. I have a million laughing-hysterically memories with Dean, as well as incredibly emotional ones, and thank God, we brought Creed into the world.

I hear people talk about hating their exes or regretting ever getting married, and I've never felt that way. I wouldn't undo or alter any decision I've made; they led me to where I am now. Getting married was the right decision for me back then.

There also came a day when ending the relationship and getting a divorce was the right decision. However painful the decision to move on was, the choice to stay somewhere I had outgrown would have caused so much more pain, on all sides. I would have played a part, I would have worn a mask, which would have caused him too as well. He wouldn't have been happy, and neither would I; our kids would have felt that. I wouldn't be growing, and growth has always been my number one core value. Sometimes couples evolve and change together, sometimes they don't, and the time comes to move on.

He had the courage to say those words, and I had the courage to follow through given many chances to give up and retreat along the way. The next two years were incredibly challenging, painful, and the most freeing. Duality breathes again.

Solitude

The second significant time of solitude in my adult life was during and after my divorce. By divine grace, I found a small two-bedroom house. The housing market was terrible, and every apartment had a three-six-month weight list. A friend of mine knew about a house that had just been mostly renovated and was about to go up for rent. She called the owners and told them about me, and I got a call the next day. She asked if I wanted to come see it and I did, praying it would work out. It wasn't my dream house; however, it was the perfect size for Creed and I temporarily. I loved the idea of not having apartment neighbors, that it had a fenced-in backyard, and I was desperate. I offered her whatever cash she needed to rent it on the spot. They posted it the night before, and she already had one hundred applicants interested. Thankfully, my friend must have spoken highly of me, that or this woman could see the pain in my eyes because she gave it to me without a second thought.

The memory of packing up my things is a blur. All I remember is Dean leaving with Creed for the weekend so I could do it, and the few friends that came to help me. I sobbed with every item I put in the boxes. I took on so much shame and guilt, crucifying myself with my thoughts.

Making everything my fault, I took on one hundred percent of the weight for it all; even things I had no business carrying. Two sweet friends went with me to get the basic things I needed for the new house and thoughtfully put everything away while I sat emotionless on the couch, struggling to function. Like a walking zombie, I felt completely empty inside.

I sold my dream car for something more affordable; I feared cutting my income in half, and learned the hard way of what happens when you put yourself in a position of having no credit. We built an incredible business, however I didn't have my name on anything, so when I got divorced, it was a struggle. Getting any car at all was challenging, and our business production dropped; partially because of the chaos, partially because of the economy.

I share this as a warning for anyone who needs it, and especially women, to be smart and protect yourself financially. I never imagined I would get a divorce, and then I did. There were many things I got to learn about for the first time, as my husband handled a lot of things I would now need to know, like the bills.

The emptiness, pain, and fear I experienced the first few nights alone in my new house I really cannot express into words. I truly felt I was dying, and a part of me was. The only thing worse than my pain was feeling my son's confusion when he would cry for his dad at night. To add to my grief, I still had to keep my business going. A cycle of forcing myself out of bed and counting the minutes to get through the day when I would go to work. My work demanded an upbeat personality, forcing me to pour out from a very empty cup. Many people turned on me and made me out to be the bad guy. From their outside perspective, I was the one who tore my family apart. For many in our community that meant I was the one that tore their family apart as well, like I ruined their lives. My relationship and my marriage became such a comfortable source of their joy to rely on, and I was selfish for taking it from them. Very few people were taking into consideration it was MY marriage and MY life, which was hard for me to understand. In a lot of unbalanced relationships, I felt like a possession instead of a person. Many of whom I once considered family threw me to the wolves. Some of which I had poured so much time, energy, and love into over the years, making it that much more painful. More than one friend going after my ex before the ink dried on our divorce papers, for one example. There were so many parts of the story no one knew, and I felt if I needed to defend my right for someone's love and respect, they didn't deserve it. I stayed quiet, observing everyone around me as if I was in a snow globe.

Adding to the pain, I found out that a close family friend had stolen thousands of dollars' worth of merchandise from my store. She had been going in the middle of the night to smuggle product into duffle bags and keeping the profit. My business partner and I became aware after setting up security cameras when we couldn't figure out the major loss in profit that had been accumulating.

I had given this person and her business a massive amount of my time and energy over the years. This person watched my child, and we had birthday parties together. Smiling and hugging to my face and draining my resources in the dark. I confronted them and cut them out of my organization and life immediately.

Lessons

Although brutal, this was another time God was cleaning house. Another time I was shown clearly who was for me, and who wasn't. I didn't retaliate. I let them all fade away in peace as I held space for their judgments and opinions of something they hadn't lived or walked through, and for the betrayal; I forgave them. Focusing on myself and my son was all I had energy for, so that's what I did.

I had lived alone before, but never with so many responsibilities, and never with a three-year-old. That first year alone revealed to me even more what I truly am made of, and I will never question by ability to rise ever again. Holding for Creed's emotions, working full time, (Dean quit the business so it was all on me to keep it afloat) and doing everything else. Showing up regardless, knowing people were talking behind my back. I had a routine of being Superwoman Sunday-Wednesday, having a full mental breakdown when Creed went to his dads, and gathering my strength to pick him back up on Friday to do it again. I suppressed many of my emotions because I needed to for survival. Sometimes the depression was so thick I felt I couldn't even change my clothes from the washer to the dryer or get out of bed if I didn't absolutely have to. I also had to learn boundaries with my ex. I was confident that our marriage was over, however; I was also grieving the loss of Dean, my best friend and business partner. It didn't take long for me to understand that he had his own pain to heal, and I had to let go of any desire to stay in touch except for what was necessary for Creed.

Divorce is painful, scary, and so incredibly lonely and the only cliché advice they give you is "time heals," and although annoying, *they* are right. There was no way out but through, and slowly I remembered who I was, what I was made of, and started coming back to life, one day at a time. Letting my old life die once again, so my new one could truly be reborn.

Angels in Disguise

An awareness I've come into is the patterns of my life. With every darkness and isolation period, there were always angels. In this season, there were the people that showed up for me. The friends that washed and put away new dishes and hung curtains when I was physically unable to. Friends that would call and check in and talk to me for hours. People who defended me, who didn't judge. A customer turned dear friend who has mowed my grass since I moved in and checked in on my safety many times with no expectation of anything in return. His wife becoming my assistant and helping me tremendously, keeping my head above water business wise. The loyal ones who stayed by my side through divorce. Family and friends that helped me with Creed and opened their home to us for holidays. My reiki coach who supported me through such a painful, weak period. My landlord coming to the rescue if anything was ever wrong with the house. The car dealership getting me a car as quickly as they could. Opportunities aligning. Angels are always there if you look for them. Even the kindness of a stranger on a day that feels insurmountable, or a song playing when I needed hope, look for the light.

CHAPTER EIGHT

A NEW STANDARD

The next relationships I care to share about interestingly enough were not relationships at all. I feel time is an illusion; There are friendships and relationships I took part in for years that didn't make half the impact of a brief conversation with a stranger, a weekend with a roommate given to me at random on a retreat in Arizona, or in this case; a brief two months where two men, in completely different ways, taught me very intense lessons. I've found everyone and everything is a teacher, and you never know which ones can change the direction of your life in an instant.

Mr. Right

I had known the first one briefly for years. Not well, just from work and in passing, let's call him Tom. The small interactions I had with him were always positive. Tom had a big smile and dimples and was always happy to see me. I never thought about him much past that because I was married and having a baby when we first met. There was a four-year period where I didn't see or hear from him at all when our organizations started working separately.

I hadn't dated anyone since my divorce and had no interest to the first time he asked me out. Tom was witty and clever and if I had been ready to go on a date; he was the kind of person I would have said yes to. I had just moved into my house and was fighting to keep my head above water, as you now know. I couldn't possibly imagine trying to go on a date while navigating the emotional turmoil I was facing, so I politely declined, to which he replied, "no worries, I understand Penny, let me know when you are ready." I loved that he called me that. No one except my immediate family and the kids I went to elementary school with called me that anymore.

That was in June. The summer passed, and truthfully; he hadn't crossed my mind again. Aside from one random day, he sent me a song at the exact moment I needed it. I had never heard it and I will never forget the experience I had listening to it for the first time. The song was *"Better days"* by *Dermot Kennedy*, and it became an anthem for my life, pulling me forward on my hardest days.

I still share it with people often because of the impact it had on me at my lowest, and I cried the most freeing tears hearing it live this past summer. I used that song as a beacon of light to survive a lot of days, and it would find its way to me any way it could. It would come on in a shoe store at the mall, or over loudspeakers at an event. There was even one time it started playing in my car at a red light without me opening any music app or even turning on the stereo.

"Better Days Are Coming, If No One's told you,"
– Dermot Kennedy

Mr. Red Flags

I was working constantly, navigating single-motherhood, and intensely training at the gym. It was early October and on this particular evening my son was at his dads. I had been in a relationship since I was fourteen years old, with very brief periods of being single, as we've discussed. The greatest demon I was facing at the time was my fear of being alone. Universe coming in hot with another lesson. This was the night I met bachelor number two. Let's call him Andrew.

The loneliness and boredom I was facing this night set me up for the perfect trap to fall into with a cute guy on Instagram showing me attention. He had been liking my photos for a month or so prior, but I had yet to pay him any mind. His name popped up in my inbox with some kind of hello and I thought, "why not?" I replied and enjoyed the fun of the banter, messaging back and forth. I had no idea who he was, had never heard of him or seen him before, and honestly questioned if he was real as he looked like he hopped straight out of a GQ magazine. Andrew appeared to be my age, and spoke a similar language through his content. He spoke of personal development, personal growth, work ethic, and from what I could tell, he was a single dad to a beautiful little girl of a similar age to my son. On the surface, we seemed similar, and I had myself convinced I wanted to "have fun, go on dates, and not fall in love with anyone." I think that's why I blocked Tom out of my head. Tom seemed serious; someone I could see myself with. Andrew was the complete opposite. Andrew felt like someone you *should* go on a date with after being married the last five years.

The thing about myself I knew then but was desperately trying to ignore was I am not, nor have ever been, a "chill, have fun, let's hangout" type of girl. I find depth and meaning in something as trivial as moping the floors of my house- I have a podcast on it if you don't believe me. I don't small talk. Anyone that knows and loves me can tell you our time together involves dissecting the complexities of life and working through a deep layer of the subconscious mind, or brainstorming ideas to make our dreams a reality. Usually, upon a first meeting with a new friend, we've either decided we aren't a match, or they have borne their whole soul to me and will trust me forever. I am a soulmate girl; A hopeless romantic who loves love. I do not do casual anything. I was trying to force myself into a societal narrative when I was designed for a different era.

In reflection, I am sad for the version of myself I was at this time. I didn't honor myself, my truth, or my intuition. I had lost most of my confidence and had little respect for my life. I was in survival mode. In a desperate energy of seeking validation, seeking love, and looking to feel something. Again, this set me up for attracting the exact type of person I got.

He demanded to take me out, and I was hesitant. I let him know I would be two hours away for the weekend for my friend's birthday if he wanted to meet me there. I offered because I was positive someone I didn't know wouldn't drive two hours to take me on a date. I was wrong.

The next month was a chilling flashback of synchronicities from my abusive relationship with Adam. The universe presents lessons, and if we do not learn, they show up until we do. In my experience not only have they repeated, but they increased in intensity each time, and although I was always learning and changing, the deep heavy backpack wounds hanging on for dear life caused me to continue calling in these relationships, but what was I not learning?

Time Warp

He love-bombed me and put on a whole façade of who he was, and of course, being in the low vibrational energy I was in, and my naïve nature -I believed him. He pretended to be kind, he pretended to be connected in his faith and disciplined in his work. He pretended to be an honest, loving father, and he pretended to be successful; portraying someone who had his life together.

One of the first mornings I stayed over at his house, he woke me up at five AM by picking me up and carrying me to the kitchen with a hot tea already waiting. On the counter, he had a journal for us to do affirmations; he played personal development, and we went to the gym. I was ecstatic, a dream come true. All the things I liked to do that most people didn't understand, he was acting like he did every day.

That was the only day that happened lol.

Thankfully for me, he couldn't maintain the fake persona as well as Adam, and the love bombing only lasted a week or two before his true nature began to show itself. A full-blown textbook narcissist.

He was manipulative, possessive, aggressive, and lied more than he told the truth. Did you ever go to a party when you were a child and have the exciting realization that there was a pinata there? You see it hanging up in the corner of the room and it's so enticing. Shaped like a cupcake or a spiderman head, you just couldn't wait to take a baseball bat to it as hard as you could, hoping to be the one to free all the candy inside? Can you picture what it looked like when someone finally busted it open, and tootsie rolls and smarties went flying everywhere? Well, I was the child, Andrew was a pinata, and all the candy? His red flags.

The first red flag being the relentless nature in which he got me to go on a date with him. He demanded it until I agreed, which at the time I mistook for "masculine energy." Number two; He took me to a haunted house, and if you knew me at ALL, you would know that is possibly the last activity on earth I would ever enjoy. To this day I don't understand why I didn't know immediately this was a screaming NO!

The first time I went to his apartment, I found he lived in an expensive place, and I knew what he did for work. The two were not adding up at all. When I went inside, I realized there were very few traces of a child anywhere. I am a single mom. I know what a house looks like when a kid lives there and how much stuff they acquire. Within a few days of knowing him, there was a story of someone "stealing a large amount of money from him," and one of the first times we went to dinner "something was wrong with his bank card" and I paid.

I share all these little things now to bring awareness to the clarity that something was very wrong. I have found so many of us do this wild thing where we completely turn off and disregard our intuition for the fun of the fantasy. This is why a strong sense of self is so incredibly necessary, and when we are in seasons of vulnerability and low self-esteem, dating is not a good idea. It really wouldn't have mattered who it was, or what screaming signs presented themselves. I was in a vulnerable state with rose-colored glasses and earmuffs on awaiting my new adventure. I was like those people in the *Scary Movie* parody where there is a large blinking sign that says SAFETY LEFT DEATH RIGHT just skipping my way right down the death path.

Plot Twist

One day we were on the phone, and I was asking what he had planned for the following night. He mentioned going to watch some fight or something at a friend's house. "You know the guy

I'm going to hang out with actually," he said. Confused, I asked him what he was talking about because I really didn't know anything about this person I had just so freely let into my life.

"Yeah, you've worked with him before I think, Tom." Still having no idea what he was talking about, I said, "Tom who?" I almost dropped the phone and thought for sure I was going to be sick. To my horror, he said Tom's last name and then continued ranting about how much he looks up to him and what a great mentor he had become for him. My mind tried to comprehend how in the hell I had managed this one. OF COURSE, Andrew was Tom's new bff I had never heard of. Why wouldn't he be? My life is quite the? Yep, movie. You remember. Goosebumps all over my body and the worst feeling in the pit of my stomach came over me when I thought about Tom. I wondered why I hadn't ever reached back out to him. I would have much rather gone on a date with Tom over Andrew, but in my weak, codependent state, I made a decision, not understanding the connection, and therefore the consequences of being involved with Andrew at all. Everything is working out for us, that I would later learn, however in the moment I was hurt, and I was at a loss.

I focused on letting go of Tom ever even being interested in friendship after Andrew went to the party. I imagined him showing a picture of me like a trophy and Tom's face shocked. It's not that I thought Tom was pining over me. I'm sure he wasn't. However, the kind and respectful nature in which he treated me to then be told I was sleeping with this random friend of his who had a reputation for treating women terribly would probably sting anyone.

I was somehow immediately trauma-bonded to Andrew. It was like I got put back into my seventeen-year-old body and relived my first relationship all over. I was extremely attached, even though everything about him was sending up panic signals in my body, left and right. I was a robot when it came to him. However, thankfully, my mom intuition never left. I never let him meet or come near Creed; (another flashing neon sign I knew he was bad news) He played every manipulative mind game possible even worse than Adam. I was meal prepping one time, and he called to ask what I was making, "It better not be anything nasty like the last time you cooked," he said, and then continued demanding I do all these things for him. He talked to me like this often, but for some reason, this comment snapped me out of my trance. "I'm meal prepping for myself. I'm not making you anything," I said in a feeble attempt to stand up for myself. He unleashed. Screaming and cussing at me, he blocked me off everything for two days. Just as Adam would, he would come back with all this fake kindness and "love" reeling my zombie self-right back. I finally woke up about a week later. This whole thing only lasted a few weeks but felt like it was much longer.

We were up late watching YouTube. Ironically, Andrew was the furthest thing from light or love, and he introduced me to two people of deep contrast to him I so deeply resonated with. The band *Satsang* and *Aubree Marcus*. I was entranced in this Aubree Marcus podcast that night and my intuition was lighting up, connecting deeply to everything they were talking about. It was a podcast he was doing with his wife, and I greatly thank them for snapping me out of whatever time warp I was trapped in. It was like two in the morning, and he was frantically and obsessively looking at his phone like you would if you were waiting for someone to text you. I asked, "Who are you waiting for a message from?"

Big mistake.

I was genuinely curious. I would dance between these very different levels subconsciously where I would channel my seventeen-year-old abuse brain, and my married -in a safe healthy relationship brain.

When I posed this question, I was asking from the latter. There was no insinuating or questioning of his character. For a reason undenounced to me when I asked, it didn't even cross my mind this would be a question to cause defense or conflict. Naïve. I had forgotten I was not in a healthy situation; I was in a situation where you didn't ask things like that. The way he yelled at me sent a chilling fear through my whole body. The anger in his eyes, his body language. I remember looking at the door as if almost finally realizing the possibilities of being involved with someone like this. I felt so much post-traumatic stress as I choked back tears attempting to fall asleep, afraid he would yell again. Part of me wished he would have hit me, because the way he would scare me then apologize shortly after saying things like "why do you have to make me do that?" felt so much more of a mental mind-fuck. Any aggressive nature he would showcase sent my nervous system back in time, reliving all of it once more.

I woke up the next morning to a note on the pillow that said something about how "peaceful" I looked when I slept, and he had gone to play football and would be back. I sobbed uncontrollably, thanking God he was gone. It was Thanksgiving Day and per my parenting agreement, one of the first holidays I spent without my son. Coming to the realization my fears of being alone had put me in a far worse situation, I woke up remembering the powerful person I am. I also woke up full of shame for somehow slipping into this alternate reality in the first place. Regardless, I was sure of one thing. I needed out. Immediately.

I got up and started picking up and cleaning things to calm my nerves, waiting on him to come back. Breaking up with a narcissist is not quite as easy as breaking up in a healthy relationship. I went to sit on the couch with a book and my foot brushed a bag under the couch. It was a DoorDash order with a receipt on the front of the bag dated for the past Sunday. There were random food items, everything in pairs of twos. The last thing on the receipt was two bags of chocolate. This was significant for a few reasons. He had canceled plans with me this day because he was "going to get his daughter." He also didn't answer me for those two days, which wasn't abnormal because he did whatever he wanted, but if I didn't text back fast enough a search party would have been issued.

The chocolate was significant because he would Door Dash food for us and would always order me the same candy. One other important detail was he had not posted any photos or videos of his daughter that weekend. Someone like Andrew ALWAYS will capitalize on a chance to show they are a "good parent." If you needed me to spell it out for you, Andrew, I had finally figured out, had a system, as most narcissists do. Narcissists don't view people as people, and they don't truly feel emotion. They see others as a source. What can you do for them? A source of money, sex, status, food for their ego, it can be many things. Regardless, narcissists tend to have a lot of sources. You make them mad or aren't giving them what they want- they go down the line of people on the list until their needs are met. I was thrilled because now I had clear proof to make my exit, and it was so blatantly obvious I was positive he wouldn't be able to fight me on it.

I was wrong yet again.

I placed the bag of trash on the counter and sat back on the couch, waiting for him to come home. He came in, smiled, and said, "Did you order food?" one finger on the bag, glancing inside.

"No, but you did," I replied, awaiting his realization.

He looked from the bag to me with an evil smile, realizing what I knew, and then, like a robot, I watched his face glaze over, preparing to lie. I started asking him questions to which he gave different answers, telling on himself more than twice until he got angry enough and turned it around on me. (For your notes, a narcissist will always make any and everything your fault.) He went cold and quiet and told me all the reasons why he was breaking up with me. I remember all this emotion welling up and wondering how he had turned it around and manipulated me so well to the point I was upset. I told him it would be the last time he ever saw me, to which he replied, "good. You're too much" and walked away to get into the shower. I stood there frozen, unable to move. As I talked about in Adam's chapter, there's a part of the human psyche that forms attachments with abusers, and I was gaining the strength to break the cycle.

I was making a promise to myself once I walked out of the door. Not only would I never see him again, but I would never allow myself in an unhealthy connection ever again. "I forgive you," I said when I walked out, to which he laughed. Again, it wasn't for him, it was for me. After this whole thing was over, I found out so many lies it blew my mind. One example for context, I found out Andrew had multiple kids. Like MULTIPLE. from multiple mothers, and a lot of mess attached to him. Andrew can do whatever he wants with his life. We aren't here to place judgement on Andrew. I was the one calling this person into my life. The real question I was asking myself was, "How did I get this so wrong?" I was losing all trust in my own intuition and discernment.

"I promised myself,"

"I promised I would never allow myself in an unhealthy connection ever again," and I meant it. I always meant it. I had been promising myself that since the first time I was treated poorly, lied to, cheated on, or talked down to. What was the disconnect? How was I replaying this broken record repeatedly, cutting myself deeper each time? The

issue was I didn't keep promises to myself. I had lost my own trust long ago. These promises were merely hopes and dreams. I had lost my integrity within myself because subconsciously I felt I deserved the treatment I was receiving. The patterns were woven so deep inside of me, something massive had to happen to wake me from my trance.

Lessons

A few days after I left Andrew's, I got Covid and was extremely sick for about ten days. I cried the whole time. Being forced into isolation demanded a strict halt to the all-day-everyday hustle I had thrown myself into since my divorce. Being an over-achieving work-acholic was how I coped, as you now have learned. Ten days alone in my house, so sick I couldn't even busy myself with chores, forced me into immense grief. I think I processed the majority of the two years prior in those ten days. If you know the kind of tears that ache from the inside out, you will know what I mean. I barely ate. This was the beginning of my journey of finally facing myself.

I had moved so quickly for eight years strait. In truth, I had been moving quickly since childhood. Filling up every minute of the day with work, with getting better, getting stronger, getting smarter, produce, produce, produce, learn, learn, learn. Shoving any pain or traumas under the rug and moving on to the next thing. The next workout, the next achievement in my career, the next car, the next trip, or the next partner. I think a lot of people were forced into a similar halt during the shutdowns, unfortunately one of the reasons we saw such a huge rise in suicide; Facing yourself is the hardest thing to do.

My business was in health and nutrition, and while many businesses struggled to stay afloat, mine skyrocketed. I worked more than I ever had in the two years when most people were at home.

Now this was my time of pause. My body forcing me into a break I wouldn't have been willing to take if I had a choice in the matter.

Clearly, I hadn't ever taken a break. I had yet to face myself in any capacity. Never allowing myself the time to look in fear of what I might find. This was the start of me getting sick a lot more often until I would learn to listen to my body screaming for rest and begging to process bottled up emotions.

Over the next two months, I dedicated myself to introspection. While receiving reiki, I worked with a coach on inner child healing, and began addressing the wounds covered in this book. Meditation transformed my life forever.

I was in this interesting limbo as I was beginning to understand myself more and more, simultaneously relating to my current world less and less, the start of my awakening.

CHAPTER NINE..EIGHT..SEVEN..

It was New Year's Eve, and I started the day like any other weekend my son was at his dad's by going to the gym, meditating, and taking a nap. I hadn't been hanging out with many people and hadn't been interested in drinking or going out. However, I was beginning to worry I was turning into a hermit. I decided I would find some plans for the evening and force myself to go out and interact with other humans. A few friends had invited me to different places. One at home with her and her kids. Being that I was already sad about not having Creed, I opted out of that one. I didn't know what I was going to do, but decided I would start getting ready, regardless. I hadn't put makeup on in a month and thought it might pick me up a bit. When I was doing my hair, a friend messaged me and asked what I was up to for the night. He told me a big group was getting a table at a nightclub in Cleveland and invited me to join. At first, it was an immediate no, then I took a deep breath, looked in the mirror and said something along the lines of "you have to leave your house to make friends Penelope."

I asked him if I knew any of the girls going because I was brave, but I was not about to go out in Cleveland until two in the morning with nowhere to sleep and one guy friend I barely knew. He told me about the girls and thankfully one of them going I had just met a few months before, so I messaged her. "Hey! I'm thinking about coming out tonight. Any way I could come meet up with you first?" I asked. She was the sweetest person on the planet and not only welcomed me, but invited me to stay with her, and even offered me a sparkly dress to wear. I was so excited to meet new friends. Most of my community were all married with kids and older than me. Now that I was a single twenty-five-year-old co-parenting mom, I was eager to meet some new people.

I finished my hair and makeup and typed her address into my GPS. When I arrived, she greeted me with a huge smile and a hug, introduced me to her sister, and we finished getting ready together chatting. All glammed up, I hopped in the back of her car up for whatever adventure awaited the night. I was ready to leave that year in the past and welcome a new one, praying for better days to come. "Where are we going?" I asked, popping my head into the front seat. "We are all meeting at Blakes. He lives downtown, we will pregame for a bit and I'll leave my car there. We can Uber to the nightclub. You remember Blake, don't you?" She asked.

I knew of him just as I knew *of* most of these people but hadn't had many conversations or interactions with them. I looked out the back window while she and her sister talked in the front seat when her phone rang. I could tell she must be talking to Blake because she started laughing and put the phone to the side to tell us Blake's apartment elevators were broken and we would get our exercise by walking up the three flights in our heels. Just before she hung up, she said, "Okay, I just have to swing by and pick up Tom and I'll be there."

"I'M SORRY WHAT." I thought. Did I mention my life is a movie? Remember Tom. Tom, that asked me on the date. Tom, that unfollowed me on all social media accounts when he found out about Andrew. Tom, that I hadn't seen in person in four years. Tom, that I had planned on never seeing again as long as I lived. Well, that same Tom was about to get in the back of a car with me at ten PM and spend our New Year's together. I fidgeted with the gold sequins on the tiny little dress I decided to squeeze myself into, and suddenly wished I had a tequila shot. He came out of his apartment, and I thought I was going to be sick. He opened the door and stood in the middle of the road for a dramatic amount of time looking at me, sighed, and said "Penny," with a big smile.

Second Chances

He slid into the backseat beside me, saying hello to my new friends. He smelled good, and my heart was beating so fast, unsure of what to do. The people pleaser in me assumed he hated me. "Hi, I'm Penelope, nice to meet you," I said awkwardly with my hand reached out, waiting for his to join it for a handshake. He stared at my hand, laughed, and shook it. "Tom," he said. I sat the rest of the ride in silence, trying to ignore the tension and thought, "once we get there it will be loud with lots of people, and we can go our separate ways." We hiked the three flights of stairs at Blakes, and I hugged the friend that had invited me. He introduced me to some of the other people joining us, and I took photos with the girls, my anxiety at an all-time high. Ironically, my homebody self couldn't wait to get out of that apartment and into a nightclub. It felt like it would be much easier to hide in a dark room with hundreds of people and blaring music.

We arrived, and I headed straight for a booth, relaxing that I had finally made it. To my shock, Tom climbed into the booth right beside me and my nervous system was officially wrecked; "What the hell is he doing?!" I thought.

He smiled at me and shook his head, laughing, looking away. "I thought you hated me," I blurted out. He scrunched his face, confused, and asked, "Why would I hate you?"

"Well, after the Andrew thing and I noticed you unfollowed me on everything."

"That definitely sucker punched me, but I would never hate you, Penny. I unfollowed you because I don't want to look at and admire you anymore. There is no chance of their being anything between us after that. He's my friend," he said.

I felt regret hearing his answer, wishing I hadn't ever messaged Andrew back to begin with.

"You and I are good, Penny, swear. No hard feelings," he said. "Good," I replied, smiling.

Suddenly Tom is all I could focus on, and to be one hundred percent honest I'm not sure if it had anything to do with him, or the fact that he implied I "had no chance" and the game of winning or proving him wrong was the real impetus. Probably a little of both.

Our eyes locked every few minutes from across the room, both a few drinks in. I never said a word, would just smile when I caught him looking at me. He started shaking his head and smiling at me until I finally yelled "What!" into the space between us.

"TWO YEARS!" He yelled back. "TWO YEARS I MESSAGED YOU AND WAITED!" He yelled, taunting me playfully as he left the circle of people and met me face to face.

There was a girl that night I later called "red dress" who wouldn't leave his side. She glared at me the whole night, but I didn't care because he was staring at me with her. He told me of how he had always admired me, and *I was the best*. He told me of how highly he would have treated me, and how he could have seen himself with me. How I was the girl to be with, one that turned all the heads when I walked into a room, and whose intelligence and wit were unmatched. I'm not sure how much of this he meant, or if this was something he told to girls all the time, however for the sake of the story I suppose it doesn't matter, I believed him and if he was playing a game, he was very good at it.

He then told me I had wasted and ruined it with Andrew. I told him I understood, and I didn't see any reason why we couldn't get to know each other now if he liked me so much. My flirting skills were at a ten if I do say so myself. We went back and forth like that most of the night, hitting a proverbial tennis ball.

Divine Protection

It never occurred to me the friend that invited me may be interested in me. Naïve Penelope yet again. Curveball for my evening. We were into some of the same things; he had just gotten out of a relationship almost the length of my marriage, and I thought he was amazing. However, something in me screamed when he surprisingly kissed me that he was meant to be a friend, and a friend only. I did my best to navigate the situation with kindness and grace while this whole drama with Tom was playing out. Thank God my intuition warned me about my friend because plot twist from the future- he would turn out to be non-other than my future love's little brother. Yikes. So interesting how divine timing works. Eli was still a mystery to me and was in Costa Rica that December, or he probably would have been there that night.

Yikes again. Oh, and Tom and Eli also used to be best friends. Yikes AGAIN.

I felt like I was playing musical chairs when Tom came back to me once again. He shared that when he found out I would be attending this evening via his friend's group text, he walked straight to the mirror, pointed a finger at his reflection and said, "You will not touch her." I remember laughing so hard at that, but he was right, not even a New Year's peck on the lips.

He kept saying with his words, we would only be friends, but the energy was telling a different story. I let him be as the night got later and spent time with the girls. Wasted per my bartending buddy, I barely had eaten anything that day and didn't drink much anymore. When I felt the intensity of the alcohol, I stuck right beside my new friends to make sure I would get home safely. Not my proudest moment, but I passed out in the uber. Her brother carried me inside and layed me down next to my best friend for the night, the toilet. I puked my life away and woke up the next morning to ten missed FaceTime calls, in her bed, not remembering what happened. That was the last time I got drunk; it was an old version of myself I let die and wouldn't be carrying with me into my future. Happy New Year.

His curiosity must have gotten to him because Tom messaged me the following night asking how I was feeling. Apparently, he was asking for me on FaceTime with my girlfriends when your girl was passed out on the tile floor. Divine protection lol.

For the next few weeks, Tom played with my emotions. Part of me wonders if he really was conflicted, or just interested in hurting me for what happened with Andrew. We would text and flirt, we would talk on the phone and talk about going on a date one day, then immediately the next, he would go back to his rules. I rode the roller coaster of our conversations. We had great chemistry, and our banter was entertaining. I could tell how much he liked me, and for whatever reason, the game continued.

One thing that came up in our conversations was a list he had made. Tom said he had really spent time thinking about what he wanted in life, and what he wanted in a partner. He wrote down qualities he would like them to have and the kind of relationship he desired. He said I checked almost every box; that part I didn't necessarily like. However, the concept taught me something. I had never taken the time to really sit and think about what I wanted in partnership. I had always made lists and vision boards for life goals and business but never taken the time to really set intention with whom I wanted to attract as a romantic partner.

One day out of the blue, he messaged me to tell me that he met someone and wouldn't be texting me back anymore. I felt defeated and sad. My ego was very fragile. Thankfully, this was well into my healing work, and I really started to step into *-things are happening for me* mentality. I focused on myself, making my own list, and then went to work on all the things I wrote down to make sure I was an equal for the partner I was wishing to attract in my future.

Games

Two weeks later, he was messaging me again. I was confused. Apparently, things didn't work out with the girl he met. I assumed if he took the trouble to start talking to me again, he must have gotten over whatever was stopping him from taking me on a date. I was wrong again. He must have been getting something from the hamster wheel we were on, which I can understand. If you desired a girl that turned you down, and now the tables were turned and she was waiting like a little puppy for attention, your ego probably would have loved it as well.

I was in Cleveland that weekend with the same girlfriend from New Year's and he texted me, insinuating I come over, following up with some comment about how it probably wasn't a good idea. It was late. My friend was with a guy she was seeing, and I was over the middle school dialog and told him to send me his address. I got there, and we sat on the couch talking for a while, conversation flowing like it always had.

The mental manipulative game he had been playing with me then went to a new level. He told me he wasn't kissing me because he knew he would never be with me, and if he kissed me, he wouldn't be able to stop. He -his words *respected me too much* to touch me in any way if he knew he wouldn't be with me. At that point, I was thankful for the clarity, but then he got close to me.

> *"Stay in your place better seen and not heard,*
> *but now that story is ending"*
> *– Princess Jasmine*

This next part is very difficult for me to write; however, I'm sharing for the person who's been through something similar and holds shame for experiencing it. I spent a lot of time going back and forth with sharing this part of my story, however hiding a truth in any way when my intention is to empower others is just not something

I will do. There was a blue jay that visited me every day I wrote this book, and still does. It shows up right in front of me on a tree branch, a fence, or even lands right beside me. I will see one fly while I'm driving or hear its call when walking in the park. It's served as a sign, from my spirit guides, God, my angels. There are so many beautiful things this bird represents and one of them is its beautiful blue color, the same as the throat chakra, and a very loud call. These birds are strong, and other birds don't mess with them. Every day I see this little bird show up, it has been a reminder to use my voice even when it is hard, and to stand strong in my truth and my story. I'm sharing for the person who didn't have the courage to stop something they knew was wrong or speak about it after. This whole book is clearing my throat chakra that's been blocked for far too long, and for anyone else who needs encouragement to let their inner blue jay sing.

Tom picked me up and brought me in front of his large high-rise apartment windows, then sat me down and leaned into me. He made comments about not forgiving himself for having me in his apartment and not "seeing me naked." I took my shirt off because he was guiding me too and acting like anyone else would if we were about to hook up. Instead, he did something so odd. He just stared at me for what felt like forever, moving his hands up and down my body, barely touching me like a cat torturing a mouse before it kills it. Moving his face close to mine, turning if I tried to kiss him, he played this manipulative control game. Smiling, he told me how great I was, and how long he had thought about this moment, while playing out this strange power dynamic and treating me like I was an object, or a possession. I was so confused by the whole thing I just stood frozen, giving away my power and dignity. In total truth, I remember standing there with thoughts of convincing him of my worth with my body. He never kissed me, but he touched me.. all over, and got off with me barely touching him. Going straight to the shower when he finished, he asked if I needed one. I felt like I needed much more than a shower to wash off the feeling I had. Why I stood there or why I didn't leave, I cannot tell you because I was so uncomfortable and vulnerable the whole time. I told him no, put my clothes back on and sat back on the couch, confused and my heart racing, still frozen. At first, I thought he was teasing and playing out some fantasy he had, and I didn't fully grasp what was happening or how messed up the whole thing was until the next day when I got home. It was the most degrading, weirdest experience I've ever had. It felt very intentional from a mental aspect. I was so confused how this sweet person was capable of behavior that felt... sinister. I had never felt more worthless, and he acted as if nothing had happened, as if he was a good guy for not sleeping with me. It only got worse.

He looked at me and shook his head smiling when he got out of the shower. I was at peace with leaving his house and this whole memory in my past, but the game that I had been drug through had me clawing for answers. I wanted to know the reasoning behind "I would never be with you." Especially after whatever the hell just happened. I told him I could handle it, I wanted the clarity, so he told me.

He first started with what I thought was the deal breaker, Andrew. He was mentoring him, and he said he couldn't see his bride walking down an aisle knowing that someone at the wedding had *been* with her. Listening; I had no interest in asking any furthering questions or debating any of his beliefs regardless of how absurd I felt they were. That one was no shock; I had been hearing about this struggle for weeks. The next reasonings, however, took the breath from my body. He talked for a much longer time, and used words to soften the blow. However, to sum it up, I was too damaged for him. The things I had shared about my life, the traumas I had overcome. The lack of generational wealth in my family- he didn't want any part of that. He had a close relationship with his married parents, and I was too messy is basically what he said. He didn't want my baggage. He also let me know he just couldn't be okay with a son in his family that was not his blood line. This one really made me pinch myself because I was sure I was dreaming. Not that I am oblivious to this is the way some people feel, because everyone is entitled to whatever opinions they have regardless of how bigoted. However, my son had been earthside the whole time Tom had been pursuing me. Creed was never going anywhere. If he had beliefs about bloodlines or whatever, I just thought maybe he would have taken me off the roster years ago. He literally even said to me it would be different if Creed was a girl. The worst part of this whole experience was after being completely defiled and listening to him rip me apart for every circumstance besides what mattered most; me as a person, he then told me how unfortunate all those things were because I, myself, was *the best*. I was number one. I had everything. I turned every head. He said, "man, whoever ends up with you will really win." I wanted to punch him in the face, cry, and laugh at the same time, but I was so tired I just went to sleep instead. When I woke up, I called an Uber, grabbed my keys, and you'll never guess; I hugged him goodbye. I knew he would never have the honor of being in my energy again and although silent, I was thanking him. He told me his truth. As harsh, cold, and hurtful the things he said were, he had the courage (or weakness) to say them, and a part of me was thankful for the fucked-up game he just put me through because it was the catalyst for change.

Rejection is divine protection. Amen.

Before this night, I had thought Tom was the exact type of person I desired in a partner. He was witty; he was funny, successful; he took care of himself, and the one that gets to me the most, he was kind.

I really should finally address the obvious epiphany I have had with my love for kindness, and for you, my dear reader, in case you relate and it's still not clicking. Serial killers can appear kind. Someone appearing kind isn't proof of anything! Lord have mercy! Back to Tom. Lol.

What I didn't know is how different our hearts were. What I didn't realize until the wee hours of that morning was I had been making decisions and operating from a surface level. I had been in this cycle for so long and so many times I couldn't see the pattern. Just like I said before, I was a puppy looking at everyone with big bright eyes, happily accepting a pat on the head or a kick to the stomach.

Ironically, I am so grateful for this terrible night, for it opened my eyes to a new level of self-worth I had not yet tapped into. I finally took ownership. Something shifted. It was *my* job to protect myself. I could talk about how judgmental and narrowminded the things he said to me were, and I could demonize him for the domineering mind games he played with me, but I won't. Tom is not the villain here, no one is. Tom clearly has his own pain and his own issues, and that's not my journey. This is my story, and in my story, I was the problem. Tom is irrelevant. I couldn't control Tom, don't you see? Hating Tom or Andrew does nothing for me. That would be reflecting and projecting more judgement! I was the common denominator in all these painful experiences. Tom was a blessing in a very twisted disguise, and so was Andrew. Tom was the proverbial straw that broke the camel's back. This was about me and my belief backpack walking into painful experience after painful experience. The way you allow someone to treat you is an accurate representation of how you feel about yourself. Remember that.

I left his apartment that morning with a newfound clarity. I was on a mission to heal. I was done dating; I was done with these men I was attracting. I was going to heal and become so happy and powerful on my own I would be able to feel if someone was for me or not. I needed to restore my intuition.

I was done with the surface. I went to work on my self-worth and my trust within myself, because there was a lot of work to do, honey. I didn't trust myself at all anymore after being SO wrong back-to-back. I was done chasing anything; I surrendered to God that I was done. I was ready to listen. I had been kicked enough.

CHAPTER TEN

THE ULTIMATE LOVE STORY

A few months passed as I poured all my energy into healing. I was meeting with my coach regularly and having breakthroughs; Journaling, meditating; I was even doing a spiritual womb cleanse, committing to clearing and cleansing every part of my past. I had reached a place of peace and comfort in being alone and had hope for my future again. My plan was not to date anyone for a year and spend that time getting to know myself. To fully focus on Creed, and get clear on who I was, and what I wanted in life. I had finally stopped focusing on love and turned the focus on myself, and just like that (the Universe has a wild sense of humor), that's exactly when love showed up out of nowhere, tearing my plans into beautiful shreds.

Now we loop back to revisit chapter one if you would like to re-read it to freshen your memory on where we left off with Elijah.

Twins

Across multiple religions, there is one common thread, and that is the belief in a soul. Regardless of your faith, many are in alignment that we all have a soul, and this body is the holding place for that soul while we are here on earth.

The soul is who we are inside. A definition from Google defines the soul as *the spiritual or immaterial part of a human being or animal regarded as immortal.* I align with this concept; I am a soul having a human experience, and my body is a temple, giving my soul a place to inhibit and experience what it is to be human. If you have an animal or a pet, you're very connected to, this is another example. They aren't just a pet; they are family. Their soul is having the experience of what it's like to be a dog, a cat, or a horse. You can feel the love and connection with your pet in a similar way that you do certain people, a kindred soul feeling.

Have you ever heard of twin souls? Whether you have ever heard of the concept or not, and whether you believe in such a thing, let's say they are real for the fun of it. The information I share in the following text is what I believe about them. There are many resources available if you'd like to do your own research and you're entitled to believe in whatever you believe in.

This is my story. Take what you want from it and leave the rest.

The concept of twin souls, or another name for it being a "twin flame" is a concept of two people sharing the same soul. One soul incarnated into two bodies on a very important mission.

This is a different concept than a soul mate or a soul family member. A soulmate or a soul family member is like the kindred souls' example I shared above. I believe we all have many soulmates and soul family members. Many people marry a soulmate. Your best friend is more than likely a soul family member as well. However, a twin is different. It is my understanding not everyone has one, and if you do, it is only one person.

A twin flame doesn't necessarily come in the form of a romantic partner and doesn't have to be "the one," although they could be. They could come in any form, and regardless, the purpose of the relationship is ultimate transformation. Regardless of the form the relationship takes, when you encounter your twin, your life is guaranteed to change and will truly never be the same.

Your twin is your mirror. Whether you knew each other growing up, or you lived separate lives from across the world, once you meet you will immediately feel at home. Once you get to know each other, you will find many synchronicities, and you will find many aspects and life experiences you've had mirrored one another.

The connection will be highly spiritual, and the purpose, as I mentioned, is one of transformation and healing of oneself with the trigger of the other. The connection to them is unlike any other could possibly be because you can feel the other half of your soul inside of them. Through this connection, the goal is for both twins to become the highest version of themselves by uncovering their worth, their strengths, and facing their deepest wounds and insecurities. Each twin is designed to trigger the other, and bring to the surface anything that needs healed, or any trauma buried deep inside. The deep love and pull towards the connection provide a dangling carrot to push both twins into facing themselves and alchemizing in the process.

I know all this now because I have been walking this twin flame path for a little over a year now with Eli. I hadn't ever even heard of such a thing and neither of us knew what we were experiencing until about nine months into our relationship. Once I came across this information and started digging for answers, I felt so much relief, as if to finally have some understanding of the wild nature of what we were going through. I read tons of different people's stories, all expressing very similar feelings and experiences to ours, and I was so grateful for some kind of explanation to go off. Understanding the path we were on helped me navigate it exponentially better.

A twin brings out the most potent love inside of you. A twin cracks you open. Your twin also comes fully equipped and prepared with every fear, insecurity, and belief you have hidden in your belief backpack and their job is to pull them all out and lay them on the table for you to heal as you do the same for them. Your love being the lighthouse guiding the ship through the treacherous waters.

Runner Chaser

You already read what happens first, soul recognition. I saw an interview where a doctor shared the more intense and stronger a pull and an attraction when you first meet a partner-the deeper the wounds connecting you. The immediate love at first sight feeling changes something within both twins at a deep level. When the pair connect, the world as they once knew it basically blows up. Coming into union immediately triggers a massive spiritual awakening in both twins, inviting a new perception of reality. Many people explain these kinds of shifts happening to them after a near death experience or losing someone close to them. Something so emotionally intense that it shakes them to their core and snaps them into a completely new reality. This was my version of that.

This explained why we loved each other immediately and the magnetic pull we felt. As I shared in the first chapter, we worked through the first few layers of our heart opening relatively easily for what was to come. Like being in a small canoe each with an oar in the water, rowing in cohesion, deepening our connection and having our "level one" hard conversations.

Figuratively high fiving each other after surviving resistance, as we sailed along, relishing in our courage and our perfect love, basking in the self- proclaimed healers we were. Back to the visual of the canoe. Imagine us smiling on a clear sunny day. Imagine us with life jackets and sunglasses on, paddling through a tranquil stream, facing the slight occasional current up against us in synchronized teamwork with both oars in the water. Now imagine the sky going black, the wind picking up; the stream going over a waterfall and into an ocean with unforgiving waves and lightning. Imagine our canoe flipped over, both of us holding on for dear life as sharks circle our boat.

This is the visual representation of the next phase of facing our inner selves we were headed into.

The deeper we got into relationship, the closer we got to our inner wounds and the closer to the flame. The closer you get to a fire, the hotter it gets, the more intense the triggers.

In a twin flame journey, it is natural for twins to take on the roles of runner/chaser as the relationship unfolds. Each twin typically spends time in both the runner and the chaser role. Per their response to their childhood wounding, they are more comfortable in one role or the other. You can probably guess I was the chaser most of the time in this dynamic. My codependence, need to people please, attachment, and bleeding heart fully qualified me for this role, especially feeling a deeper love than I ever had before. His inner-child wounding response set him up perfectly for the runner. To protect himself, he would form a little shell around his heart and create distance for the fear of the pain it would cause to let it in and then lose it. What I find so interesting is our very similar childhood experiences created two very different trauma responses. My trauma response turned me into a love bug. His response turned him into a crab, burying himself deep for protection. I martyred myself for love. He kept love at a distance, both of us desiring safety. We both needed to heal the same wounding, it just manifested in two different ways. Two perfect ways that would trigger the other to the point of no choice but to heal it, or if the fire was too hot, to leave the connection.

The only way to stay connected was to stay in the fire and handle all the pain and fear that came up. As a result of this kind of intensity, times of separation have been an integral part of our path.

For the remainder of this story, I will only be sharing my side, for as I've shared in all my other relationships, this story is about my experience and my growth. My partner's story is not mine to tell. My perception of his story would be just that, *my* perception.

The Letter

I let you go. *I let you go because the desire for sleep finally surpassed the desire to be wanted or chosen by you. I let you go because I wanted air more than I desired to feel your touch, because your touch was accompanied by waves and drowning. I let you go because the knots wrapped so tightly around my hands and my heart trying to hold on to you were causing cuts and the dripping of my own blood on the ground was enough to startle me back into truth. What is it that I was so strongly holding on to? Was it the unconditional love I had always dreamed of? A connection so strong and so deep no one else could possibly understand? The kind of love where you can hear each other's thoughts, feel each other's pain? A love where I felt seen, cherished, honored, appreciated, worthy, and safe?*

The answer is no; it wasn't.

Although that is the illusion I created around what my soul feels for yours. The divine, unexplainable connection and opportunity to heal ourselves and the story I could so clearly see was just that at the end of the day, a story, a lesson. Potential I saw glimpses of in our own private world, but what about the real one? The truth is I know and exude that love. The love that would do anything to keep you safe. To protect your heart, your peace, your happiness, your growth. To keep you from any pain, to serve your highest good, even if it meant not getting what I wanted. My love feels so foreign to you and at times I could feel you questioning it, "What's the catch?" there wasn't one. This is what true love is, no agendas or games.

This relationship with you and I wasn't going to work on this timeline because I love you more than you know how to love yourself. The truth is you never protected me from pain. You caused it. You didn't honor me the way I always honored you. You were fighting your soul. Simultaneously, I was fighting for your soul.

I let go of the need to be seen, to be wanted, to be chosen by you. I choose myself. I will protect my heart the way I fought to protect yours. I was holding on so tightly to being waiting. To be put on the back burner, forgotten, left out, uninvited, unsafe, and lied to. This block holding you back from facing your shadows, causing your heart to be closed and continuing in these patterns, is no longer in alignment, so I had to let you go. You should also know I forgive you completely. I let you go in light, and love. I let you go rooting for you. I see you. A light I feel no one else truly understands, and I hope you can find a love within yourself as strong as I have for you and heal, being with me no longer being the endgame. It is why we are here, and as painful as this has been, it won't be easier next time. I won't be here next go-around because I choose to listen, and to face it, my heartbreak being a huge catalyst. Thank you. The sound of our laughter...time stopping when you looked into my eyes...the kind of love that could only break your heart completely open once it was gone.

You have the power to set yourself free. I will always be somewhere believing in you, even though it will look much differently than I thought.

Attachment

I wrote that letter to him during a three-week span we went without speaking, beginning in January. He read it in a hotel room sitting across from me, both of us sobbing. It was the longest we had gone without each other, a lot leading up to this point. Reading that letter now, there is truth behind my words, however there is also a lot of wounded patterning and projecting I can only see now as I have healed so much since then. The line "because I love you more than you know how to love yourself," I believe was true. However, it was only true because he was my mirror. I, too, didn't know how to love myself. That letter was my inner five-year-old screaming at him for the pain I didn't know what to do with, and I let her out in the hotel room that night. I felt I was doing all my work, and he wasn't doing his, not realizing the biggest part of my work was to release any attachment to what he was doing, period.

There was so much love there that the process of releasing my attachment made me feel like I was physically dying.

I have now grown comfortable with death. It is a crucial part of the alchemical process. The version of myself that needed him, anyone, or anything else needed to go for me to step into the highest version of myself and get rid of my backpack once and for all.

"I died as plant and rose to animal. I died as animal and I was human. Why should I fear? When was I less by dying?"-Rumi

"*In an unhealthy attachment, one person typically looks to another for emotional support, usually without offering much in return. The partner who consistently provides support without getting what they need may feel drained, resentful, and unsupported,*" according to Google.

You can hear in my words this is exactly the stage we were in. I was looking to him to fix it and stop the pain I was feeling. I was drained, resentful, and unsupported.

It was one of the darkest three weeks of my life, a new level unlocked. The heat got too hot for me to handle and something he did triggered and hurt me so badly I cut him off.

He then became the chaser; this is how it works. He sent messages, videos and songs continuously reaching out, none of which I received because I blocked him. I loved him so much. If I saw any of it, I would have been right back. When someone has deep fears of the unknown, one way they tend to cope is by staying in a pattern because the certainty of how a story ends is comforting, even if it's painful, and even if they are no longer fulfilled by that ending. We could go into these separations until brought face to face and the love and the pull to one another would force us right into another cycle. I wanted a different ending, so I was willing to take my chances.

Alchemy

We would have a beautiful week or sometimes two falling deeper in love and one of us would bring up something big to work through.

The first few weeks these conversations were not that bad. (Sunny day in the canoe). They were usually around things like him being unsure of his future. He was unsure of where he would live, and how much he would be traveling, which sent up panic signals for my fear of abandonment that I was forced to face.

Other things like the dynamic with his ex, who was now his best friend, who refused to acknowledge my existence; and me bringing my interesting past to light, challenging every part of our egos. Like Tom, and my random encounter with his brother on New Year's, for example. *Face palm.

Apparently, those were things he expressed were necessary parts of slicing open his insecurities, as his were mine, and much later when I read all this twin flame stuff, I felt a lot clearer about the tangled web we weaved. We would spend hours navigating, usually a million tears, sometimes one would need space, but I don't think we ever quite made a twelve-hour period without deciding we weren't going anywhere.

The more time passed, the deeper our connection, the more intense the conversations. (The dark sea) There came a clear point where our soul connection was unbreakable, and simultaneously our physical relationship was not healthy, and I fought that knowing as long as I could. He was clear on what he could give, and what he couldn't. I was also clear on what I wanted, what I could give, and what I was no longer (and never should have been) okay with. Like many times before, I started sacrificing my boundaries for love.

I won't speak on Eli's reasoning, again that would be his story to tell, however, how it manifested was an extremely private life which I wanted at first. My marriage had been very public, and I really enjoyed our life just being ours. There came a point, however, where I was ready to be free. Freedom has always been, and will always be, my top priority alongside growth, and I will do whatever I have to do to maintain that. I started feeling the same caged feeling and denied it as long as possible for fear of losing the magical bond we shared. I also could feel he wasn't being honest, and the trust started to break.

On Repeat

I was never afraid to express whatever was happening for me once I realized it. By this point we knew we were in this together regardless of if that meant we would stay in a relationship or not.

We were both clear that the love had far outgrown the container we had it in, and we either needed to move forward into a bigger one or set each other free to grow on our own, and we tried. We tried many times. Understanding something logically and getting your heart in alignment are two very different things. One of us would be strong in leading a breakup, while the other processed anger and pain, eventually coming to terms with the decision. All to be completely thrown out the window after staring at each other on FaceTime and saying forget it! We passed back and forth the runner chaser roles like a football. I don't know how many times one of us drove in the middle of the night to the other one after lasting two days on our new solo paths. We took turns in this cycle for the next six months. Universe says evolve or repeat and we chose REPEAT.

In all fairness, each time we went through another cycle, another level of healing or awareness about ourselves came through, and the connection deepened time and time again. The thing about the spiritual nature of our connection is although from the outside it could appear toxic, we never were battling each other. The pain and anger were always towards the parts of the path we didn't understand. We were never "fighting and breaking up." It was always fighting what we knew we had to do. Fighting the knowing of clearing a karmic cycle out, fighting ourselves, or our fear of doing what we needed to, to become the highest versions of ourselves and align.

We faced a million things, and he pushed deep pressure into every wound I had repeatedly.

We were stuck in a loop. I finally decided I could only control myself, and I was ready to take the chance on a new ending like I shared above. This is what led me to the letter. I deserve the world; it was a part of my lesson to remember that.

One of my steps to come into true self love was coming to terms with no matter how much I loved him, and no matter how strong the connection, the relationship wasn't healthy. I knew I deserved better. Part of my growth was gaining the courage to accept and come to terms with what I knew, hold my boundaries, walk away, and get off the boat.

The Lessons

This is where the empathy conversation comes back around. I had to learn that just because I understood his pain; I understood his fears; I understood his trauma; I understood his soul, and the path we were on, was not a reason to continue accepting his actions. This is where, "I love you, and I can no longer stay here" must come into play, compassion being the compass.

Compassion is my compass.

Liberation of self, while still holding a compassionate lens is the truest way to love someone else because as I said earlier,

We can only truly love someone to the extent we love ourselves.

The lesson for me at this part of the journey was that of finding my own power within and realizing it had been there all along. My power wasn't something I needed to learn; it was something I needed to *remember*. I was coming into the realization that I had been giving it away in every relationship my entire life and taking on roles that were never meant for me. Another very difficult discovery was realizing that although the love was so big, giving my power away in my relationship with Eli wasn't any different.

What I understand now is I had a big problem with receiving. This resulted in attracting relationships where I would give way more than my partner. Leaving relationships like this was difficult because my partners were usually very satisfied. Why wouldn't they be? I would have drowned to keep them breathing, even after realizing they were the ones trying to drown me.

I stated above our relationship wasn't toxic, however, there were many ways it was, as painful as that is to admit. I loved him so much I chose to blind myself from all the ways I was disrespected. The truth is I didn't feel it was toxic because I had faced such extreme mistreatment in my past that the ways I was being devalued here were so different in comparison. I never questioned how Eli felt about me when we were alone. It was out of our bubble that caused the pain.

Every time I wasn't included or invited, I gave my power away.

Every time he walked past me in public and pretended I wasn't there, and I allowed it, I gave my power away.

Every time he came home to me after those occurrences, and I allowed it, I gave my power away.

Every time he poured his heart out to me, and told me I was everything to him, and I allowed words to compensate for his hurtful actions, I gave my power away.

Every time I stopped myself from posting pictures I wanted to, every time I silenced myself, or hid how I felt, I gave my power away.

Every time I went back, crossing my own boundaries, knowing I wasn't okay with the way things were, I gave my power away.

Every time he hid the truth, and I ignored it, I gave my power away.

Every time I bent the truth to people around me or defended his actions, I gave my power away.

Every time I protected his feelings above my own, I gave my power away.

Every time I was poorly treated around, or by his friends, and I allowed it, I gave my power away.

Every time I sat in an audience, listening to him speak as if the things he was speaking about weren't lessons we were growing through together, pretending like I didn't exist, I gave my power away.

When I was asked by some random fan to hold her coat so she could take a photo with him as I stepped to the side like a groupie, as if I hadn't been his partner for an entire year at that point, I gave my power away.

Every time I took my clothes off, every time I got back in his bed, back in his arms, back in his soul, I gave it all away.

There is quite a difference in connection- soul recognition-love, and partnership, in my opinion. One can so deeply admire another, feel an unexplainable connection, *and* not be prepared to care for that connection in a partnership. There are a few things necessary for the kind of partnership I desire. A true partnership in my eyes is far from easy or perfect. I know there will be times in the tranquil stream, and there will be times of great storm. I desire a partnership that is filled with growth and bringing out the best in each other. One that holds space for that growth to happen. I am up for whatever could be thrown at us, however; I need to know the person in my boat has my back to feel safe enough to brave the storm. I need commitment, truth, and freedom. If I don't have that, I don't have safety, and without safety, I can no longer be in the boat. The imagery is one of fighting the rough waters. Frequently looking over my shoulder, paranoid my partner is going to jump out of the back of the boat. If we were Jack and Rose on the *Titanic*, I need to know my partner would at least have the decency to scoot over to attempt to save me from freezing to death!

I have come to this clarity in what I need in partnership because I have found a love and safety within myself that no longer would participate in anything less.

These are non-negotiables because when I enter partnership, it will be a choice that is adding value to my life. I have gained the courage and awareness to accept only what I desire and am willing to give equally in partnership, or I am at peace on my own. My peace and honoring my worth are now a number one priority, and I will not betray myself again.

The most difficult part about writing this part of our story is the intent. I have many theories on Eli and all of them are compassionate.

I know to the depths of my soul hurting him would never be my intention. So much so, I came close to sacrificing the final step in my healing by not sharing my story. You're reading this because I came to terms with the only way I could ever reach the pentacle of true unconditional love in another, was to first see and honor it within myself. As my twin is my mirror, any work or healing I do within myself energetically supports him on his journey and vice versa.

I had to realize I had the power to love myself in the way I had always wished for someone else to. I had to release him from the responsibility I placed on him. I had to release him from conditions. I saw a meme, I'm not sure who to give credit to, but it said,

"Sometimes you have to make a decision that will break your heart but heal your soul."

The truth is, I am the love of my life. Until I really believed that nothing else would fall into place.

You are the love of your life

I share this intimate story because I want you to know that the right choices in our lives are often difficult to make. The road less traveled. Often healing something means undergoing an emotional or spiritual surgery of opening, or causing a gaping wound before it has the chance to heal correctly.

Imagine you injure yourself while at work and begin having severe pain in your left knee that doesn't go away and progressively worsens. Imagine continuing to walk to work and go on a run every day regardless.

You've always loved to run. It's always been your solace. It's a functioning knee and you can't imagine being stuck in a bed and having to take a year off from something you love so much so you decide you can manage and choose to live with it. You deal with discomfort and continue to manage it however long you can with whatever numbing agents will help. Pain meds work pretty well, and a knee brace really takes the edge off. Imagine living that way for ten more years. Imagine getting to a point the pain is so bad you cannot walk. The pain in the left knee causing you to overcompensate with the right and now your right hip is beginning to ache due to the lack of balance. Fifteen years go by and now you're in for a double knee and hip replacement and possibly in a wheelchair indefinitely because of the damage, now also dealing with an addiction, because your body got so used to the pain medication. Your spouse now helps you out of bed in the morning and most simple tasks are challenging. They help you into the car to go watch your son at his college track meet, and tears well up in your eyes out of both pride in your son, and loss of the ability to do what you loved.

Now let's rewind to the beginning when the injury began. Let's say it was past the point of rehabilitation naturally and you needed surgery. This time you got it. Let's say it was an extensive one, and they had to slice you open deep. It was painful and there were a lot of stitches. You had to give up running for about six months, and it took a little over a year to build your strength all the way back. You went through some painful therapy that challenged you every day, but you got it back. You healed.

Now it's fifteen years later and you enjoy a morning walk with your partner. You ride bikes with your granddaughter, and you run with your son when he's home from school training for his next season. You have the same tears of pride, this time accompanied only by joy and fulfillment of your beautiful life.

This is a law of the universe; you can see it everywhere. A person typically pays the cost of nutrition and fitness or later pays the cost of hospital bills and medication. The discipline of money management or the cost of financial stress and struggle later. The courage and discipline to follow the voice of your heart and your dreams, or to be fated to the voice of deep regret for not. Jim Rohn taught me that.

I had to decide to let go of what I wanted in the moment, to truly heal. Everything is always happening for us, and if something isn't aligning, there is a greater reason at play.

I was deciding in every area of my life to get the surgery, so to speak. Rip me completely open so I can heal, because the second scenario? The chance at living the most fully, and the freest, is always worth the temporary discomfort, in my opinion.

When I started this book, I felt so clear about my intention. Tears ran down my cheeks as I had awoken to my purpose and what I was destined to heal, the lesson I was meant to learn. I remember the pride I had that morning, as if I had finally cracked the code. I was going to share my story, my *journey back to self* and teach and inspire people how I had healed my heart and came into worthiness. What I wasn't coming to terms with was the fact I still had seven months of back-and-forth lessons with my partner after "drawing my line in the sand." Every time we would fall back into a cycle, the attachment got stronger. We were on a merry- go-round, and that version of us wasn't ever going to get either of us our desired outcome. In truth, I made many "lines in the sand." I never wanted to be without him. I don't want to mislead anyone that finds themselves in this kind of pain that this is an easy task to choose yourself. I had to fight myself over and over again until I honored my line once and for all. I can't express to you the amount of love and attachment I had with Eli through words. It's impossible to translate, and the strength to leave it took everything in me.

There comes a time in a relationship you must gain the courage to ask;

"Are we meeting heart to heart, or wound to wound?"

This kind of breakthrough and generational healing doesn't come easy. If it did, you wouldn't be reading a book about it. No one lines up to watch a football game with only one team and no defense. "Twenty-seven touchdowns, no tackles." No. Lol. Resistance, struggle, defeat, triumph that's what makes it a game.

I was forced into a fire so hot I had no choice but to be completely melted down. There was no chance of going through this journey and coming out the same on the other side.

CHAPTER ELEVEN

SPIRIT LEAD ME

I alluded to the spiritual awakening I was experiencing briefly earlier in the book and have chosen not to go deep into all of it because I plan to go in depth on my experience in another book. Briefly, I have uncovered many gifts within myself the last two years, such as clairvoyance, clairsentience, clairaudience, and a strong ability to channel through something called automatic writing. To support the lessons in this book, I will share a few visions and channeled messages that I received during meditations.

Spirit lead me where my trust is without borders
Let me walk upon the waters
Wherever You would call me
Take me deeper than my feet could ever wander
And my faith will be made stronger
– *Michael Ketterer*

Around this time, I did a guided mediation calling in a spirit guide. I was beginning to trust my inner guidance and intuition stronger and stronger as time went on, and I did these types of meditations often. I listened to the voice on the app asking me to imagine walking through a green pasture and seeing a waterfall. As the voice painted an image in my mind of walking towards the waterfall, I felt a strong presence and saw someone standing just underneath it in the distance. As the audio trailed off, guiding my own experience to unfold, I saw myself walking closer to reveal the guide that had come through. It was Jesus, or Yeshua. I connect to him so strongly and he often comes through in my meditations. Here are the notes I have from this specific meditation.

Jesus: "I am the way, the truth, and the life and so are YOU. If this was right, you wouldn't worry, you wouldn't question. How does your body feel? I know you love him, but trust in me, trust you are being guided."

I then describe the teddy bear image. If you've never seen it, there is a painting of Jesus and a little girl with two teddy bears. The little girl is clutching her teddy bear, and Jesus is in front of her with one arm outstretched, asking for her to give it to him. What the little girl cannot see is behind his back, Jesus is holding a much bigger teddy bear, and he is asking for her to trust, have faith, and release.

In my meditation, Jesus was asking me to surrender. He was asking me to release my grip, and to trust in the higher plan.

"You are the sorcerer," Jesus said.

"So, what do I do now? How do I let go?" I asked.

"You must stop viewing people and things for what they could be and take them for what they are. His actions are showing you."

In my meditative state, I felt a massive weight on my head and Jesus said, "this is what you will continue to feel carrying things you aren't meant to. The relationship is unbalanced. This does not equal the peace, love, and freedom you are convincing yourself it does.

When I ask for the teddy bear, trust in me enough to give it to me, and you will be blessed. You are highly protected and divinely guided. You can still love this teddy bear, release any guilt or shame, it's okay."

And just like that, he was gone.

As my spiritual journey has unraveled, I've come to understand more and more that we already know. We know what to do, we know when something is right, we can sense when something is off, we just must have the courage to clear out the noise, and to listen and hear the answer. I find Jesus's message so profound as I always read in the bible "I am the way, the truth, and the life," however many times I have heard in my meditations "I am the way, the truth, the life, and so are YOU." I choose to take that as we are all one, and we can possess and access the love and wisdom of God at any time we choose to. I feel he was empowering me to trust in faith, the universe, God, mother earth, and infinite wisdom because as he said, "you are the sorcerer." We all are a piece of that divinity; it is not outside of us. He was asking me to trust that all will be exactly as it's meant to be. Surrender. Release your grip, and trust.

Release

What I didn't see coming was that writing the book was its own journey in itself. You see, awareness and practice are two separate things. Do I believe this book will help people? Of course, I do. However, what I have come to know and believe is I was called to write this book to heal *myself*, and only when I gained the courage five months later to let go of my teddy bear the entire book came out in a matter of a few weeks. The time spent in solitude and self-reflection over each pain, and every experience made me realize I had never given myself that time before. I had never sat with the pain and looked it in the face. I added one experience to the next, one attachment to the next, using the next person or obsessive pursuit of accomplishment to numb the pain of the last hurt. The hurt of the last relationship was easy to bury once I had the excitement of new love. Like a little kid shoving toys they don't want to clean up under their bed I was doing the same with any trauma around self-worth. At some point the room must be cleaned.

I had done this so long I created belief patterns that I needed to be loved and successful to feel I deserved to be here. Writing this book called me into the most important lesson I feel we can learn as humans: surrender. Surrender to the divine flow and release the unnecessary anxiety that comes with believing we have complete control.

With every page I wrote, new things would surface, and I had to surrender to each of them. Pain, grief, attachments. The greatest being releasing my attachment once and for all in this final love with Eli.

I believe God gave me lessons to learn, with each experience intensifying until I got it. I was faced with scenario after scenario, presenting me the chance to change my beliefs I acquired in my backpack decades before. *Excessive overthinking, fear, people pleasing, a "never first" mentality, over achiever, perfectionism, trust issues, fear of being alone, I need rescued* all falling under the same umbrella of self-worth and self-love.

With each relationship, I gained strength. I gained knowledge. I got the strength to walk away eventually, but I never truly learned the deep lesson of unconditional love and self-worth until this one. Talking the talk is much easier than walking the walk. I've been practicing affirmations for years, however, this was a belief so much deeper, and so strongly ingrained inside of me it was almost impossible to find and felt even more insurmountable to truly face.

It took my own mirror in a person to serve as a catalyst. It took a connection I never thought possible, and a love I started to believe I couldn't live without for me to finally face it. It took the person I loved most not treating me the way I knew I deserved to be treated to let go. I finally had the epiphany no one was supposed to choose me, I was supposed to choose myself, and in doing that, it would create a ripple effect in those around me to choose themselves. I had an epiphany that the healthy love and partnership I desired would require me choosing myself, and my partner choosing themselves, allowing the space for a healthy connection free of codependence and wounded patterning. One of the hardest things I've ever done was the act that finally set me free. When I finally let go of the attachment, I was forced into surrender. I felt every ounce of pain in doing it, and I sat in it every day I wrote this book and months after. I healed. I took the weights out of my backpack one by one and remembered how to stand up straight.

Mike, the artist from the concert we went to on our first date, has a song that says,

"*The only person I ever lost and needed back was me.*" An interesting full circle moment for me, and hopefully a line for you reading this to fully absorb. That's what writing this book has become for me. A version of myself having to die completely for the chance to be reborn. Put so deep into a flame I had no other choice but to melt away all the things no longer serving me, and then rising from the ashes like a Phoenix. The version of me that attracted unhealthy connection after unhealthy connection is gone now, and I fought like hell to get rid of her.

Channeled message from Jesus

"I am asking for the teddy bear now and for you to trust the next step in the process of trusting your intuition, what you see, what you hear, and what you know. There is no reason to doubt your prophecy or actions when you feel directly pulled subconsciously or consciously. You are being led and divinely guided towards your destiny, dear one. Trust in me and I in you. Put your faith in me and I will show you the way. This world and life you have created in your mind is the small teddy bear you so tightly cling to your chest. Let go, release. Close the door on what is not for you to create the space and make the way for us to bless you. Feel into your heart space. Know and trust your guidance. Your gifts and the path you have been trained and prepared to walk, my child. I in you, we are one. You are clothed in Christ consciousness and equipped by your ancestors and spirit team to bring light. The only way to go forward in truth is to honor yourself and come to terms with change is a constant, and acceptance for each corner and turn in the road. Feel into your resistance, feel into your pain, and trust in your knowing, your faith, and your optimism that you are deserving of light. You are deserving of healing, of abundance, unconditional love, and the free will gifted to you at this time in history to create the life, peace, and the prosperity that calls you. Step into the call and trust what is for you cannot be missed or mistaken. Trust in the free fall and excitement, releasing fear of the unknown and attachment to your past and move forward in strength, peace, courage, love, and light. That is all for now.

Re-read, breathe, be with the earth and ground in what you know to be true, not what is attempting to come through in fear. What do you know when you feel into your heart, wind on your face, and spirit ever present around and supporting you? Aho, Amen."- Yeshua.

CHAPTER TWELVE

HEALING

As for my twin and I, I listened to an interview Ed Mylet did with John O'Leary in the midst of this journey that forever changed my perspective on us, and how I view love in general. If you aren't familiar with John O' Leary, he wrote the book *On Fire*, a book where he shares his survival story of being a burn victim when he was a young boy. The burns were so severe it was a miracle he made it. He shares an emotional story about the first time he shared dinner with his family after the fire. He talks about sitting in his wheelchair at the table surrounded by his siblings and parents struggling to pick up his fork to eat his potatoes. He had lost the majority of his fingers and was expressing how impossible it felt to get the food from the plate into his mouth. His sister stopped eating and went to help feed her brother when something miraculous happened. "Put it down," his mother ordered his sister. John then shares in the interview how his mother demanded he learn to feed himself, and she would sit there with him until he did. He expressed the anger, rage, and betrayal he felt in that moment. He was a victim and felt his mom was so cold. He said it took hours, but eventually he figured out a way to hold the fork and eat. He then shares how in that moment, with the help of his mother, he got his power back. He went on to live a very happy and successful life. The interview is called *Victim to Victor*.

John's mother knew unconditional love. She understood the best way to love him was going to hurt them both in the moment. Can you imagine the pain of watching your baby, that had just faced unimaginable pain, stress, countless surgeries, deep sadness, and loss, crying in a wheelchair and unable to feed himself? Can you imagine having the strength to refuse to help him? Majority of mothers would have rushed to his side and fed him forever, but he never would have learned to eat on his own.

Unconditional love is truth, and truth sets us free. Unconditional love is doing first what is true and best for yourself because that is the only way to serve or love anyone else authentically. It is not our weight to carry how anyone else feels about our truth, it is only our job to speak it. I almost didn't share a story that changed my life forever because of the love I feel for Elijah. Not sharing this story would have been my version of feeding him, or my version of being fed. A true soul agreement is one that encourages the other to heal and grow. However they are guided, regardless of the trigger it causes in the other.

The story of the fire changed how I love myself, how I operate in partnership, and how I parent. I want to be the partner, the mother, the daughter, sister, or friend that says, "put it down," and I want the same done for me.

The best way I can love my twin is to show up authentically in love and, truth. Navigating our relationship in whatever form it takes and he can only do the same for me. We have free will, and our healing and futures are not reliant on the choices the other makes. We are on our own individual paths, learning to feed ourselves regardless of our connection at a soul level.

Our programming of love may lead you to feel let down that this story didn't end with a white horse and a wedding. However, that is the exact programming I was called to shed light on and heal. The happy ending is one of self. One of "the girl took her power back," one of true joy and fulfilment inside. A heart in the pursuit of freedom; free of shame, guilt, regret, and attachment.

I understand some will read my story and judge, I understand some will read my story and think I am a "whore," or I have lost all my marbles; however, I do not write this story for them. I write this story for the version of myself who needed it. I write this for the person in deep pain. I write this for the person desperate for love. I write this for the person who is lost or feels alone. I write this for the person looking to write a new story for themselves. I write this story for the little girl that felt she wasn't good enough, or the woman trapped inside of the emotions of her inner little girl. I write this story for the person reading that can hear their inner voice, whether screaming or a faint whisper. I write this for the person ready to come home. I write this for the person that is awakening to their gifts and is scared or feels alone. I write this for the person ready to come back to their self. The person looking to free themselves from their limiting beliefs, their traumas, and their fears. The person who wants to embody their fearless optimistic child they left somewhere along the way. I write this for the person who needs hope, courage, strength, or a friend.

We all have a higher consciousness and intuition we can tap into whenever we are ready to surrender. That intuition and higher guidance will take you exactly where you are meant to go as mine has. It will take you on a wild journey, one of the utmost fulfillments. One of freedom.

A Journey Back to Self

CHAPTER THIRTEEN

ROSE COLORED GLASSES

What a beautiful perspective I wrote our story from. A loving, genuine, very true for me-perspective. What a romantic concept? A twin flame. A connection so deep, so magical, and so genuine, I was *absolutely* sure of it. I was also POSITIVE he would never lie to me or hurt me. What if I was wrong? What if it was all just a story? Is it possible the idea of a twin flame connection is just a theory I attached to? A theory I created with rose-colored glasses on. What if there were many things I didn't know? What if there were lies and deception and truths hidden away from me? What if the person I consistently put on a pedestal of divine love, and a divine counterpart, was the ultimate teacher of me learning a lesson in naivety? Is it a possibility? Is it *possible* the great love I was experiencing was a toxic attachment?

Before you get worked up, I don't know if any of that is true either. Here is the point.

I am not sure of the truth, but I have learned to question it. To be open to the possibility that I could be wrong, and in any situation, there's a chance things are not only as they seem. I've learned to see things from all sides, and from every angle being attached to nothing. I am positive about the connection I feel to my partner in this story. Could he be my twin? There is a high possibility, but I am not sure the way I was when I wrote the chapter before this one, and really the point is it doesn't matter if twin flames even exist. Attachment is attachment. Being attached to anything isn't freedom, especially if it keeps you from growth or peace in any way. An edit I took out of the previous chapter was a line I said, "I am positive to the depths of my soul he would never do anything to hurt me." I realized I was wrong about that. An epiphany within myself; The only "to the depths of our soul" intentions we can be positive of are our own. He could be my twin, or maybe a twin flame was a label I clung to, keeping me in an unbalanced relationship paralyzed from moving forward for the belief half of my soul lived somewhere outside of me.

We would sleep clung to each other most of the time. Me laying on top of him heart to heart, my arms and head wrapped around his neck like a little monkey, his arms wrapped around me. I used to view ours as the greatest love of all time, and now without the glasses, I see two very hurt, scared, children. Two children holding on to each other for dear life bonded at the soul level no matter how much their human adult versions hurt each other in the process of healing. My love has never changed, however now I love us both with clear eyes.

We are in control of our beliefs. I feel we should explore them all and go with the ones that feel good for us, even if society views them as delusional.

I believe this book will help millions of people.

I don't care if anyone else believes it. It is a belief that has fueled me to pour my soul out onto these pages, and I am allowed to believe whatever I want to, and so are you. If at any time the beliefs we are holding don't feel good for us, or are keeping us trapped, we can choose different beliefs. Holding on to a "twin flame" label regardless of how accurate it felt chained me to fear of living. Fear of living without him, fear of loving anyone else, fear of losing each other and not making it back together like my life and our love was the final level, and we needed to defeat Bowser or none of it had any meaning.

Sometimes we build our own prisons with our belief structures.
What's exciting about that is we can take down the walls
of our prisons with new beliefs that feel better.

The old belief was my partner was my twin, and his soul and mine were cut down the middle. He was my divine counterpart I came here to find. I believed I would suffer if we weren't together, and I shut off my heart from the possibility of ever having a loving connection with anyone else, and let me be honest, I thought I couldn't possibly live without him at times. This belief gave all my power up to the actions of my partner. Let's say he chose the same belief; our relationship would be extremely codependent and the love would be so fragile. Let's say he didn't. I would be waiting and accepting whatever crumbs he gave me. I would be in constant pain, putting a pause on my life for when he could be what I *needed* him to be.

My new belief is our souls remember each other in a magical, special way. This backs the otherworldly experiences we have had and how sensitive we are to one another. I believe we came here to find each other, to support one another in our growth and our highest good, to push one another into our greatest healing.

Remember when I said I believe Eli, and I made agreements before entering this life? What if that agreement planned for the exact pain I went through so I could heal? What if we were playing out some karma in this life that required me to take my power back? What if heartbreak *was* the agreement? What if our agreement was to love each other forever? What if, with our gifted freewill Eli wasn't ready? What if, when I wasn't being treated the way I deserved to be, my guides had finally had enough of watching it and took matters into their own hands to protect me?

What is true? Who is to say? I'm not sure but let me tell you what is true. When we enter this life, we forget all our soul agreements. This is why taking on a belief that everything is happening for you is a powerful one because one belief, *a twin flame romance novel* belief, leaves me broken inside, and the belief that transformation and walking away was always the plan, gives me peace.

I believe whatever the agreement, I will love Elijah always. His existence and our short time together changed my life. No matter what he does with his future, and no matter what I do with mine, whatever the reality, the love remains. That is what unconditional love is after all, isn't it?

I also believe that boundaries when needed are not only my right but my responsibility, and I can set them when something doesn't feel good or healthy for me anymore.

I believe I have the choice to make choices that feel best for me. I believe I am meant to be loved, cherished, and respected in this lifetime. I believe I have other soulmates or divine counterparts I will love, and be loved by, as I believe so does he. I believe the best is always yet to come, and what is truly for me would never miss me. Trusting I am deserving of all the love and joy in the world will guide me there. I believe spirit is always divine in her timing.

Relationship in my eyes is freedom. Choosing to love and be loved freely, truth being the north star.

What are the beliefs you hold that are imprisoning you? Where do you have rose-colored glasses on?

Is there a possibility you could be wrong? Is it possible the food you love most is the food making you sick? Is it possible the faith you feel is saving you is giving you anxiety, creating fear, and making you feel guilty? Is it possible to love and experience love from God in different ways? Is it possible the one person you think you couldn't live without, you were only meant to love for a season, and if you let go of the past, a beautiful new love could have the space to enter?

Here's the thing, like I said, I don't know. However, it's worth the question. By asking the questions and being open to new possibilities,

I have found beliefs that feel better. I have found freedom that is available to all of us. I ask you to ask questions. I ask you to explore. I ask you to explore prayer and new activities; try new foods, listen to different music, have conversations with people in other cultures. You may just find beliefs that feel better. Regardless of what anyone tries to tell you, no human being KNOWS the truth. They just believe more strongly in their truths than you do. This book is an invitation, a reminder, a permission slip that you can believe and love and think however you want to, and what is *"right"* should feel good. Unconditional love feels free. It doesn't feel like you're drowning or in a cage. My pain has made me wise; my heartbreak has made me strong. You, my dear reader, have the choice what this all means. Make it mean something beautiful, something magical.

What's Next?

I am not sure what is next for me in the form of love and relationship. However, I am sure of one thing. I am at peace within myself. I have done and continue to do the work, and I will never again silence my voice, or release my power for love in any form. Whatever is next for me in relationship; family, friendships, or sacred partnership, will be in alignment. They will be with people who are on a path of taking responsibility for their own growth, holding space for mine, and committed to truth, committed to *love*.

Because at the end of the day, what else should any story be about once you really get down to the core of all things that mean anything in this life?

1 Corinthians 13:4-8

Love is patient, love is kind. It does not envy, it does not boast,
it is not proud. It does not dishonor others, it is not self-seeking,
it is not easily angered, it keeps no record of wrongs. Love

does not delight in evil but rejoices with the truth. It always protects, always trusts, always hopes, always perseveres.

Love never fails

Poetry

Below is a poem I wrote for Eli at the beginning of writing this book.

Eli

You illuminated my world.
I now experience the sun differently.
The moon will be forever sacred.
Water is forever anointed, and
Fire burns with a new intensity.
Birds sing sweeter than I remember before, and
even the wind holds a new sensitivity.
Music has become a holy prayer:
A soul moving experience.
I now view my body as a temple, and
My presence as a gift.
I value each moment for the magic it is, and
I honor my power and my light first and foremost.
I see me now because I had the courage to first see you.
I trust in you.
I will look for you in every lifetime.
I pledge you my truth, always.
Te Amo baby

I came across this file and re-wrote the poem, to my past self this time.

Penelope

You illuminated my world.
I now experience the sun differently.
The moon will be forever sacred.
Water is forever anointed, and
Fire burns with a new intensity.
Birds sing sweeter than I remember before, and
even the wind holds a new sensitivity.
Music has become a holy prayer:
A soul moving experience.
I now view my body as a temple, and
My presence as a gift.
I value each moment for the magic it is, and
I honor my power and my light first and foremost.
I see me now because I had the courage to first see you.
I trust in you.
I will look for you in every lifetime.
I pledge you my truth, always.

Te Amo *Penelope*

The greatest lesson was discovering I held my own power all along. Let this serve as a reminder, so do you. Remember, everyone is a mirror.

The Process

Although I had unknowingly been on this journey my whole life, the process of writing carried me further than I could have anticipated. As I shared, I received the idea for this book in January and truly didn't dive into the process until late April. I wrote the first draft of this book in a month's time, and in that month I naturally and intuitively shed the layers of my old skin that were still hanging on. I gave myself the space to retreat from the busyness of the world with the intention of getting my thoughts on to paper, and as I did that something beautiful happened. I came home. I came home to myself more and more with each passing day without even realizing it at first. I disconnected from my social media platforms and silenced my notifications. I released the need to always be available and constantly update the world with my whereabouts. My phone stayed on do not disturb much of the day.

The first thing I did every single morning was go outside. I stood with my feet in the wet grass, my face towards the sun, and would thank God for another day. I listened to the birds greet me with their songs and felt deep, immense gratitude for the awe and beauty that nature and creation truly are. I gave myself space. I gave myself time. Barefoot, deep breaths filling my diaphragm and grounding myself into the present many times during the day.

I spent a lot of time in meditation, guided with my eyes closed, or sitting outside watching the way the wind and the trees would communicate. Connecting to my higher consciousness more and more in the process. I protected and cleared my energy daily. I wrote in a gratitude journal every single morning expressing vast appreciation for everything I had, and everything around me, thanking spirit profusely. The blue jay flying into my backyard at least once a day as if to check in and keep me on track. I took care of nourishing my body. I didn't plan to make any of the following changes, I just peacefully surrendered to the natural flow that was emerging. I stopped eating meat, and as I write this, I'm closer to vegan than even vegetarian, although I don't feel attached to any labels. I craved whole foods and took solace in the time to prepare clean, healthy meals for Creed and I. I ate a lot of fruit and drank a lot of water. I ate with no care about tracking macros or getting abs. With no thought, I found myself separating recycling into a separate bag when I had never recycled before. I suppose subconsciously remembering my love for the earth was reminding me that I had a desire to take care of her. I took the 60 seconds it took to free a spider that made its way into the kitchen instead of mindlessly crushing it with a shoe. Everything began feeling like a prayer. I became present to the light coming through the window as I chopped vegetables for dinner, or the way the water sounded when washing my face. I saw myself truly in the mirror and loved the person staring back at me for the first time in a very long time. I got rid of my eyelash extensions, my nails, I stopped wearing any makeup, and even stripped my hair of years of black hair dye. Nothing wrong with any of these things, and I'll enjoy them for fun in the future, but I released the need to change myself in any way. My skin cleared completely on its own, the acne I had suffered from for years, gone. I connected on a spiritual level to music and would sing and feel the words so deeply as I processed each memory and emotion I wrote in this book. I danced around my house the way I had spent the majority of my childhood- hours in our front living room pretending I was a ballerina. I got back into my body. I stretched, I danced, or did yoga every day, feeling into how strong the vessel carrying me truly is, and what a magnificent temple I have. I grieved all the time I spent not treating my body like the gift it is and vowed to never shame it again. Every time I would catch a glimpse in the mirror when getting out of the bath I would pause and appreciate the fortress that had carried me twenty-seven years through it all, and a body that created life and gave birth to a son. I connected to my divinity and my sexuality without it being attached to anyone else's approval.

I released my grip on anything that I no longer related to, whether that be big things like what my future career would look like, relationships that were one sided, or smaller things like certain brands or the clothes I wanted to wear. I released my labels. I released expectations. I released the things I had taken on as a part of my identity that had overstayed their welcome. I no longer felt the need to explain myself or to perform. I desired a slower life, so I created one. Perhaps one of the greatest gifts I received was as I connected deeper within myself, with the earth, with the present, I released my thoughts from focusing on things I couldn't control and opened my heart for deeper connection with my son. I experienced him with a newfound clarity. I listened to the songs he would sing and watched his facial expressions like a movie while he would build Legos or play with his monster trucks. I stared into his sparkling eyes as he would tell me a never-ending story about school or what he did at his dad's house over the weekend. He danced with me; he sang with me, from time to time he would even meditate with me. We took walks every day, and I would run beside him as he rode his bike without training wheels. I was present. I took such appreciation in each mundane moment. I poured love into him each morning routine instead of stressfully hustling him out the door. I felt the love ripple through my body when he would run and jump into my arms yelling, "mommy!" when I picked him up from school. We made sandcastles and watched sunsets together, ice cream cones and the windows down. I stepped back into the role of his mother instead of his friend. I chose to step back into a disciplinarian; I had lost that for a few years while attempting to survive. I gained my respect back with my child, telling him no, and sticking to the consequences when he would test me. I read to him, I colored with him, we painted and made pottery. I watched him play his first t-ball game, beaming with pride when he stopped a grounder and threw it to first base. I played Pokémon cards with him while waiting on our food at a restaurant instead of being in constant distraction on my phone. We prayed and did affirmations, and I kissed his sweet little face goodnight as I marveled at the light and pure love that he is. I listened to his laugh and held his hand in the car with the understanding that I wouldn't have this version of him for long. I created a sanctuary of safety; I created a home, inside and in the 3D. I got comfortable in my aloneness when he was with his dad. I faced my resistance, and my fears on the rough nights, and found a safety I could create within myself, without the need of someone else to hold for me.

I took the time to call my parents more often; I took a trip home instead of reasoning I was too busy. I read a book and took a nap when I was tired. I skipped the gym if I felt my body needed it or took a walk outside instead of intense weight training, if that felt right. I stopped eating when I was full. I got lost in a good movie instead of scrolling social for hours. I stood up for myself and set boundaries with others. I also set boundaries for myself. I released resistance and stepped into a flow state. I embraced my feminine energy and finally let her lead me. I created. I wrote. I cried. I laughed. There were days I would write for seven hours straight. Sometimes my body would wake me up at three am and I would get out a full chapter, and somedays I would sleep in until ten. I stopped distracting myself. Instead of riding the waves of craving and missing someone, I stepped into the role of the observer, allowing myself to feel emotions when I needed to, but no longer reacting from a place of need and desperation or being consumed by them. I chose myself completely and truly, for the first time. I finally realized I was first. I learned to love and respect myself in such a way that I will never need to learn the harsh pattern of lessons I shared in this book again. I built a thick layer of sovereignty within myself, while maintaining my heart in its pure nature. I leave this book free, open for all the experiences that are to come.

Transformation

We love the analogy of a butterfly, however for this story, I resonate more with that of a peacock. Peacocks are known for their captivating feathers. However, here are some things you may not know about them. They are not born with their feathers; they develop as they evolve. Peacocks also eat poisonous plants. They eat poisonous plants and alchemize them into magnificent beauty. At the end of all mating seasons, peacocks shed their feathers. Only for them to come back more beautiful the next season. Spiritually peacocks represent transformation, new beginnings, self-expression, confidence, and beauty.

I have evolved. I have eaten my fair share of poison, and I have shed my feathers many times. I go forward to new beginnings with my feathers radiating and outstretched, and I invite you to do the same.

I invite you to take all the poison in your life and transform it into beautiful feathers the world will be in awe of. I invite you to wear them proudly, without shame of how you got them as you continue growing on your journey. You are the one who can alchemize all the pain and all the false beliefs. You are the peacock, moving forward in confidence, beauty, and grace. It has been within you all along.

The Work Continues

A few things came up for me in the editing process I care to share here because I feel they are important. The first being the realization that the work is continuous, the work will be forever.

Healing is not a road of perfection, but one of compassion.

Uncovering pieces of ourselves and healing is an ongoing process, and each phase is exactly how it should be. I really work on keeping an observer role instead of being a fixer, because my automatic response has been to fix all things broken, especially when I've perceived *myself* as broken.

You are not broken.

In my observation, another layer of an inner child wound was brought to the surface that I hadn't processed until after finishing this book. Naturally, my soul has a bit of a chaotic energy. A little wild child deep within me. My soul desires a bit of spontaneity, it likes a bit of edge. I've realized that per the beliefs I took on during my childhood, I made that part of me "wrong" or "bad." I've suppressed that part of myself and lived my life from a "tightly wound" place much of the time, the perfectionism being an example. While editing this book, I noticed this hidden pattern and how it has manifested so many times. I would go so hard, remain so focused, and stay in line so much to the point the wild energy had no choice but to boil to the surface, resulting in me doing something irrational and impulsive just to get it out. Sometimes not that big of a deal, like cutting my hair, for example.

Sometimes this energy would work to my benefit, like launching and starting a podcast in a week's time, and sometimes to my detriment, creating problems in my life. For example, being so perfect for so long to being a party girl overnight. Staying in a toxic relationship and bottling up the pain for so long until I impulsively moved out of the state without warning. Getting married so quickly, being a workaholic or not taking any breaks. Playing a perfection role in my marriage, to asking for a divorce and recklessly dating someone else in the process. This energy has been the source of my struggle with eating disorders as well. Perfectionism met with rebellion. In relationship I would love until my heart was bleeding and would do anything for my person until I reached a threshold and my cut off game became as strong as iron. Writing this book for an example; I stopped my life on a dime (besides being a mom of course) and wrote this whole book in a month with little to no breaks- Impulsive. I was so obsessed with business and success, and lived such a fast life for so many years to wake up and realize I desired a much different lifestyle, a much slower one. I flipped my world on its head, dropping my CEO energy and stepping into my creative feminine nature from zero to one hundred. I can have an all-or-nothing mentality, and it is a coping mechanism I created to survive. The impulsive, chaotic nature isn't even the true source of the "problem" if you want to call it that, because now that I am aware of it, I can make different healthier choices in my life to let that energy out to play, without it having to go to the extremes it has in the past. Controlled chaos if you will. What I do to myself after the fact is the issue and the unhealthy pattern I'm currently healing; one I feel, unfortunately, many will relate to. I beat myself to the ground for every decision I've ever made. Writing this book took me through so many emotions because I was faced with my inner bully, ready to tear me to shreds for everything I've ever done, and every mistake I've ever made. I have been my own worst nightmare for the majority of my life in the form of my thoughts, and I've had an epiphany. I have unforgivingly torn myself apart for things I've done that stemmed from the coping mechanisms I acquired, from painful things I experienced, that I had no control over. WE CANNOT CONTROL WHAT HAPPENED TO US.

Essentially, we beat ourselves up and carry extreme pain and guilt for things we have done in response to coping mechanisms we didn't even realize we had caused by traumas we couldn't control. Also, the beliefs about what is right and wrong are subjective rules we learned. I have come to terms with the fact that I have done the best I possibly knew how to do in every stage of my life, and I am done carrying judgement for any of it. I am so much more than my story. Who I am now is completely different than who I was 5,10,15 years ago, and who I will be 5,10,15 years in the future, and THAT IS THE POINT. True freedom is owning every stupid mistake you've ever made, making peace with it, and thanking it for the lessons it gave and where it brought you too today. This realization is why I have the confidence to send this out into the world. I am unattached to these past versions of myself. I am also unattached to the past versions of everyone in this book. We are all here to learn. We are all here to grow. If you choose to do better with knowledge once you receive it or not is your choice, as we have free will. I choose to. I choose to grow and learn and honor the battered and bruised wings I have because they have carried me to the here and now. I forgive myself, and in forgiving myself I offer you an invitation to forgive yourself as well. Once we come into acceptance and forgiveness of ourselves, it becomes easier to offer the same kindness and compassion to others. True acceptance and forgiveness births unconditional love, and unconditional love is how I believe we truly change the world. No guilt, no shame, no regret.

If no one has told you today,

I Love You,
– Penelope

Better days are comin'
If no one told you
I hate to hear you cryin'
Over the phone, dear
For seven years runnin'
You've been a soldier
But better days are comin'
Better days are comin' for you
So when the night feels like forever

I'll remember what you said to me
I know you've been hurtin'
Waitin' on a train that just won't come
The rain, it ain't permanent
And soon, we'll be dancin' in the sun
We'll be dancin' in the sun
And we'll sing your song together

We never miss the flowers
Until the sun's down
We never count the hours
Until they're runnin' out
You're on the other side of the storm now
You should be so proud
And better days are comin'
Better days are comin' for you
So when the night feels like forever

I'll remember what you said to me
I know you've been hurting (is our time ever soothing?)
Waiting on a train that just won't come
The rain, it ain't permanent (is our time ever soothing?)
And soon, we'll be dancing in the sun
We'll be dancing in the sun
And we'll sing your song together

Your story's gonna change
Just wait for better days
You've seen too much of pain
Now, you don't even know
That your story's gonna change
Just wait for better days
I promise you, I won't let go
I know you've been hurting
Waiting on a train that just won't come
The rain, it ain't permanent (is our time ever soothing?)
And soon, we'll be dancing in the sun
We'll be dancing in the sun
And we'll sing your song together

Better Days- Dermot Kennedy

ABOUT THE AUTHOR

Penelope Rose is a 28-year-old single mother, author, poet, intuitive channel, and healer. She has studied personal growth, human psychology and spirituality for the last 10 years devoting herself to growth, healing, and transformation. She has gained wisdom and connected closer to the divine with a passion of communicating and sharing that healing with others through her writing. She has done and continues to do the deep work to heal the painful experiences she's had through childhood, abuse, divorce, and heartbreak. She's alchemized those experiences and turned them into an opportunity to fulfill her life purpose, to serve as a teacher and guide to support humanity with her gift.

Printed in the United States
by Baker & Taylor Publisher Services